THE FUTURE OF IRANIAN TERROR AND ITS THREAT TO THE U.S. HOMELAND

HEARING

BEFORE THE

SUBCOMMITTEE ON COUNTERTERRORISM AND INTELLIGENCE

OF THE

COMMITTEE ON HOMELAND SECURITY HOUSE OF REPRESENTATIVES

ONE HUNDRED FOURTEENTH CONGRESS

SECOND SESSION

FEBRUARY 11, 2016

Serial No. 114–53

Printed for the use of the Committee on Homeland Security

Available via the World Wide Web: http://www.gpo.gov/fdsys/

U.S. GOVERNMENT PUBLISHING OFFICE

21–525 PDF   WASHINGTON : 2016

For sale by the Superintendent of Documents, U.S. Government Publishing Office
Internet: bookstore.gpo.gov   Phone: toll free (866) 512–1800; DC area (202) 512–1800
Fax: (202) 512–2104   Mail: Stop IDCC, Washington, DC 20402–0001

COMMITTEE ON HOMELAND SECURITY

MICHAEL T. MCCAUL, Texas, *Chairman*

LAMAR SMITH, Texas
PETER T. KING, New York
MIKE ROGERS, Alabama
CANDICE S. MILLER, Michigan, *Vice Chair*
JEFF DUNCAN, South Carolina
TOM MARINO, Pennsylvania
LOU BARLETTA, Pennsylvania
SCOTT PERRY, Pennsylvania
CURT CLAWSON, Florida
JOHN KATKO, New York
WILL HURD, Texas
EARL L. "BUDDY" CARTER, Georgia
MARK WALKER, North Carolina
BARRY LOUDERMILK, Georgia
MARTHA MCSALLY, Arizona
JOHN RATCLIFFE, Texas
DANIEL M. DONOVAN, JR., New York

BENNIE G. THOMPSON, Mississippi
LORETTA SANCHEZ, California
SHEILA JACKSON LEE, Texas
JAMES R. LANGEVIN, Rhode Island
BRIAN HIGGINS, New York
CEDRIC L. RICHMOND, Louisiana
WILLIAM R. KEATING, Massachusetts
DONALD M. PAYNE, JR., New Jersey
FILEMON VELA, Texas
BONNIE WATSON COLEMAN, New Jersey
KATHLEEN M. RICE, New York
NORMA J. TORRES, California

BRENDAN P. SHIELDS, *Staff Director*
JOAN V. O'HARA, *General Counsel*
MICHAEL S. TWINCHEK, *Chief Clerk*
I. LANIER AVANT, *Minority Staff Director*

———

SUBCOMMITTEE ON COUNTERTERRORISM AND INTELLIGENCE

PETER T. KING, New York, *Chairman*

CANDICE S. MILLER, Michigan
LOU BARLETTA, Pennsylvania
JOHN KATKO, New York
WILL HURD, Texas
MICHAEL T. MCCAUL, Texas *(ex officio)*

BRIAN HIGGINS, New York
WILLIAM R. KEATING, Massachusetts
FILEMON VELA, Texas
BENNIE G. THOMPSON, Mississippi *(ex officio)*

MANDY BOWERS, *Subcommittee Staff Director*
HOPE GOINS, *Minority Subcommittee Staff Director*

CONTENTS

THE FUTURE OF IRANIAN TERROR AND ITS THREAT TO THE U.S. HOMELAND

Thursday, February 11, 2016

U.S. House of Representatives,
Committee on Homeland Security,
Subcommittee on Counterterrorism and Intelligence,
Washington, DC.

The subcommittee met, pursuant to call, at 10:00 a.m., in Room 311, Cannon House Office Building, Hon. Peter T. King [Chairman of the subcommittee] presiding.

Present: Representatives King, Katko, and Higgins.

Mr. KING. Good morning. I thank each of you for being here. Sorry I didn't get a chance to talk to you beforehand, but Mr. Higgins and I were comparing notes up here and—2 great minds get together——

[Laughter.]

Mr. KING. But there are 3 greater minds down there. But, anyway, I want to thank you for being here. The Committee on Homeland Security Subcommittee on Counterterrorism and Intelligence will come to order.

The subcommittee is meeting today to hear testimony from 3 distinguished experts regarding the future of Iran's use of terror proxies and what threat these networks pose to the United States.

I would like to thank the Ranking Member for his support in putting this hearing together and, of course, thank the witnesses for being here today. Now I recognize myself for an opening statement.

At the outset, I just want to put on the record that I strongly oppose the Iranian nuclear agreement. I believe it is a false deal, which gave Iran $100 billion, access to global markets, and greater freedom of movement.

This morning, we have seen even more evidence of Iran's true nature, as they released sensitive, embarrassing photographs of U.S. sailors during their illegal detention in Iran. This is the type of action you expect from an outlaw nation, not a nation which has just entered into an agreement, which has elements of good faith in it. To me, it is an indicator of the real thinking behind the leaders in Iran.

Since the deal was signed, the administration has basically apologized to the regime, improperly altered U.S. law to allow certain travelers that have been to Iran and other terror hotspots to come to the United States without getting a visa.

While the White House and State Department have been moving forward with the Nuclear Deal, intelligence professionals in and

(1)

out of Government have been consistent that Iran and its proxies still pose a significant threat.

Just the other day, in his testimony before the Senate Intelligence Committee, Director of National Intelligence James Clapper, acknowledged that Iran is, "The foremost state sponsor of terrorism and employs the Islamic Revolutionary Guards, Quds Force, Hezbollah, and other proxy groups." Director Clapper added that, "Iran and Hezbollah remain a continuing terrorist threat to U.S. interests and partners world-wide."

Similarly, the most recent State Department Country Report on Terrorism noted that, "Iran's state sponsorship of terrorism worldwide remains undiminished." The National Counterterrorism Center public website notes that Hezbollah, "has established cells world-wide."

It lists a number of plots across the globe linked to the group, including the 2008 plotting by a cell in Baku, Azerbaijan, the late-2008 disruption of a cell in Egypt, a disrupted operation in Turkey in 2009, and, in early 2011, Israel warned its citizens of several Hezbollah plots against Israeli interests in Turkey, Azerbaijan, Georgia, and Cyprus.

In July 2012, Hezbollah exploded a bomb on a bus in Bulgaria. Not included on the list are the 1985 hijacking of TWA flight 847 and murder of the American, Robert Stethem, and the 2 bombings linked to Hezbollah in Argentina in the 1990s.

Let us also remember that Iran has held a number of senior al-Qaeda leaders since they fled Afghanistan after the 9/11 attacks. Whenever it suits Iran, they release some of these terrorists, including Muhsin al-Fadhli, a senior leader of al-Qaeda-linked Khorasan group, who was killed in a drone strike in Syria, and Sulaiman Abu Ghaith, who was Osama bin Laden's son-in-law, who is now serving a life sentence in a U.S. prison.

Given these threats, it is imperative we examine how the administration's Joint Comprehensive Plan of Action will influence Iran and its use of terrorist proxies. While the deal is intended to prevent Iran from developing a nuclear weapon, as DNI Clapper noted in his testimony, Iran's, "military and security services are keen to demonstrate that their regional power ambitions have not been altered by the deal."

The deal is far more likely, I believe, to reward Iran, its bad behavior, with billions of dollars and improved international standing. While the administration is praising itself for completing this agreement, Iran is likely to exploit every opportunity to either weaken the few restraints the deal places on them or using their new-found wealth to further destabilize the Middle East.

We must analyze the effect this agreement has on Iran and how its proxies will change their behavior. New income from renewed foreign investment and access to funds previously seized by the West will absolutely be used to support terrorist networks. How will these groups invest this money, and does the United States face an increased threat as a result?

No. 2, Tehran will certainly provide additional resources to Shiite militias fighting on behalf of the Assad regime in Syria and to the Assad government directly. Despite the President's insistence that he wishes to see Assad go, he has negotiated an agreement nearly guaranteed to comfort Assad, by ensuring that his benefactors in Iran have the resources they need to support his government.

Does this deal reduce the likelihood that we will be able to end the Syrian civil war and destroy both the Assad regime and the Islamic State of Iraq and Syria? Will the Shia militias again pose a threat to U.S. personnel in the region?

One of the most obvious concerns is the fact that our major regional partners, especially Saudi Arabia and Israel, are threatened by an Iran no longer burdened by sanctions. How will they respond to increased and better-funded Iranian aggression?

All of these questions are urgent. I have called this hearing today to begin to find reliable answers to inform Congress and the next administration on how to best prevent Iran and its proxies from threatening U.S. interests and the homeland.

Today, we have witnesses that will provide insight as to what to expect in the coming years from Tehran and their allies. I look forward to hearing from them and thank them for their time.

[The statement of Chairman King follows:]

STATEMENT OF CHAIRMAN PETER T. KING

At the outset, I want to express my strong opposition to the Iranian nuclear agreement. It is a false deal that gave Iran $100 billion, access to global markets, and greater freedom of movement.

This morning, we have even more evidence of Iran's true nature as they released sensitive photographs of U.S. sailors during their illegal detention in Iran.

Since the "deal" was signed, the administration has apologized to the regime and improperly altered U.S. law to allow certain travelers that have been to Iran and other terror hot spots to come to the United States without getting a visa.

While the White House and State Department have been moving forward with the Nuclear Deal, intelligence professionals in and out of Government have been consistent that Iran and its proxies still pose a significant threat.

In his testimony before the Senate Intelligence Committee on Tuesday, Director of National Intelligence James Clapper acknowledged that Iran is "the foremost state sponsor of terrorism" and employs the Islamic Revolutionary Guard Corps–Quds Force (IRGC–QF), Hezbollah, and other proxy groups. Director Clapper added that, "Iran and Hezbollah remain a continuing terrorist threat to U.S. interests and partners world-wide."

Similarly, the most recent State Department Country Report on Terrorism noted that, "Iran's state sponsorship of terrorism world-wide remained undiminished . . . ".

The NCTC's public website notes that Hezbollah "has established cells world-wide," and lists a number of plots across the globe linked to the group, including the 2008 plotting by a cell in Baku, Azerbaijan, the late-2008 disruption of a cell in Egypt, a disrupted operation in Turkey in 2009, and in early 2011 Israel warned its citizens of several Hezbollah plots against Israeli interests in Turkey, Azerbaijan, Georgia, and Cyprus. Also, in July 2012, Hezbollah exploded a bomb on a bus in Burgas, Bulgaria. Not included in the list are the 1985 hijacking of TWA flight 847 and murder of American Robert Stethem, and the 2 bombings linked to Hezbollah in Argentina in 1992 and 1994.

Let us also remember that Iran has held a number of senior al-Qaeda leaders since they fled Afghanistan after the September 11 attacks. Whenever it suites Iran they release some of these terrorists, including Muhsin al Fahdli, a senior leader of al-Qaeda-linked Khorasan group who was killed in a drone strike in Syria, and Sulaiman Abu Ghaith, Osama bin Laden's son-in-law who is now serving a life sentence in a U.S. prison.

Given these threats, it is imperative we examine how the administration's Joint Comprehensive Plan of Action (JCPOA) will influence Iran and its use of terrorist proxies. While the deal is intended to prevent Iran from developing a nuclear weapon, as DNI Clapper noted in his testimony, Iran's "military and security services are keen to demonstrate that their regional power ambitions have not been altered by the JCPOA deal." The deal is far more likely to reward Iranian bad behavior with billions of dollars, improved international standing.

While the administration is patting itself on the back for completing the JCPOA, Iran is likely to exploit every opportunity to either weaken the few restraints the deal places on them or using their new-found wealth to further destabilize the Middle East. We must analyze the effect this agreement has on Iran and how its proxies will change their behavior.

New income from renewed foreign investment and access to funds previously seized by the West will absolutely be used to support terrorist networks. How will these groups invest this money—and does the United States face an increased threat as a result?

Tehran will certainly provide additional resources to Shiite militias fighting on behalf of the Assad regime in Syria, and to the Assad government directly. Despite the President's insistence that he wishes to see Assad go, he has negotiated an agreement nearly guaranteed to comfort Assad by ensuring that his benefactors in Tehran have the resources they need to support his government. Does this deal reduce the likelihood that we will be able to end the Syrian civil war and destroy both the Assad regime and the Islamic State of Iraq and Syria? And will the Shia militias again pose a threat to U.S. personnel in the region?

One of the most obvious concerns is the fact that our major regional partners, especially Saudi Arabia and Israel, are threatened by an Iran no longer burdened by sanctions. How will they respond to increased and better-funded Iranian aggression?

All of these questions are urgent. I have called this hearing today to begin to find reliable answers to inform Congress and the next administration on how to best prevent Iran and its proxies from threatening U.S. interests and the homeland.

Today, we have witnesses that will provide useful insight on what to expect in coming years from Tehran and their allies. I look forward to hearing from them and thank them for their time.

Mr. KING. Now I recognize the Ranking Member of the subcommittee, the gentleman from New York, Mr. Higgins, for his opening statements.

Mr. HIGGINS. Thank you, Mr. Chairman.

Over the past 2 years, negotiations, debates, and intelligence reports of Iran's nuclear program have largely overshadowed the regime's status as the most dangerous state sponsor of terror in the world.

With nuclear negotiations dominating the discussion, fewer and fewer conversations are being had regarding Iran's creation, funding, and continuing support for Hezbollah. As Congress continues to move legislation, provide resources, and maintain our vigilance over the chaos that has erupted in the Syrian civil war, Iran continues to support the Assad regime.

Iran is continuing to support a regime that has massacred hundreds of thousands of its own people. While I am aware of the current intelligence reporting assessment that Hezbollah's North American activity may be limited to fundraising, this is not reassuring.

What is more, this reporting is a warning that we must remain vigilant and take the necessary precautions to keep our communities safe. We cannot forget that, with Iranian support, Hezbollah has conducted numerous attacks against U.S. facilities, persons, and interests abroad.

In 1983, 241 American servicemen were killed when a truck bomb destroyed their barracks in Beirut. In 1988, Colonel William Higgins, a U.S. Marine involved in a U.N. observer mission in Lebanon, was kidnapped and murdered.

In 1992 and 1994, bombings of Jewish cultural institutions in Argentina, which Iran was directly implicated. In 1996, a car bombing in Khobar Towers, the U.S. military residence in Saudi Arabia, which killed 19 U.S. servicemen.

There is no doubt that Iran's terrorist ties extend beyond the Middle East to the Western Hemisphere, where, in conjunction with Hezbollah, it is engaged in fundraising, illicit financing schemes, and several devastating terrorist attacks. We cannot afford to be complacent. These activities constitute a real and continuing threat to our National security.

In 2011, before this very same subcommittee, with many of the same members you see here today, we heard expert testimony that Hezbollah was active and present in 15 American cities in the United States and 4 cities in Canada, including Toronto, which is 90 miles from my district.

Today, there will be a lot of discussion of the Joint Comprehensive Plan of Action, otherwise known as the Iran Nuclear Agreement. As we engage today, I hope that we can have a serious dialogue about the dangers of Iran using an improved economy to fund its terrorist proxies across the world, and the United States' role in preventing these dangerous actions.

I think we can all agree that issue is both complicated and delicate, and there were trade-offs that we had to make. Ultimately, I believe the agreement provided the United States with an opportunity to halt Iran's nuclear weapons program, and, thereby, prevent a nuclear arms race, which would have overtaken the Middle East.

The nuclear agreement provides the best viable option we have to block Iran's pathway to a nuclear bomb. It is imperative that we continue to check Iranian influence around the globe and thwart future attacks. I look forward to a robust discussion with our witnesses today.

We especially want to thank our witness, Mr. Saab. He and his wife welcomed their first child this week.

Thank you for appearing before us today and congratulations.

With that, I will yield back.

[The statement of Ranking Member Higgins follows:]

STATEMENT OF RANKING MEMBER BRIAN HIGGINS

Over the past 2 years negotiations, debates, and intelligence reports over Iran's nuclear program have largely overshadowed the regime's status as the most dangerous state sponsor of terror in the world. With nuclear negotiations dominating the discussion, fewer and fewer conversations are being had regarding Iranian's creation, funding, and continuing support for Hezbollah.

As Congress continues to move legislation, provide resources, and maintain our vigilance over the chaos that has erupted in Syria's civil war, Iran continues to support the Assad regime. Iran is continuing to support a regime that has massacred hundreds of thousands of its own people. While I am aware of the current intelligence reporting and assessments that Hezbollah may only be fundraising in North America, it is not reassuring.

What's more, this reporting is a warning that we must remain vigilant and take the necessary precautions to keep our communities safe. We cannot forget that with Iranian support, Hezbollah has conducted numerous attacks against U.S. facilities, persons, and interests abroad:

- In 1983, 241 American servicemen were killed when a truck bomb destroyed their barracks in Beirut.
- In 1988, Colonel William Higgins, a U.S. Marine involved in a U.N. observer mission in Lebanon was kidnapped and murdered.
- The 1992 and 1994 bombings of Jewish cultural institutions in Argentina, in which Iran was directly implicated.
- The 1996 truck bombing of Khobar Towers, a U.S. military residence in Saudi Arabia, which killed 19 U.S. servicemen.

There is no doubt that Iran's terrorist ties extend beyond the Middle East, to the Western Hemisphere, where in conjunction with Hezbollah, it has engaged in fund-raising, illicit financing schemes, and several devastating terrorist attacks. We cannot afford to become complacent. These activities constitute a real and continuing threat to our National security.

In 2011, before this very same subcommittee with many of the same Members you see here today, we heard expert testimony that Hezbollah was active and present in 15 cities in the United States and 4 cities in Canada, including Toronto, which is 90 miles from my district. Today, there will be a lot of discussion of the Joint Comprehensive Plan of Action (JCPOA), the Iran Nuclear Agreement.

As we engage today, I hope that we can have a serious dialogue about the dangers of Iran using an improved economy to fund its terrorist proxies across the world and the United States' role at preventing these dangerous actions. I think we can all agree that this issue is both complicated and delicate and there were trade-offs that we had to make.

Ultimately, I believe the agreement provided the United States with an opportunity to halt Iran's nuclear weapons program and thereby prevents a nuclear arms race, which would have overtaken the Middle East. The Nuclear Agreement provides the best, verifiable option we have to block Iran's pathway to a nuclear bomb.

It is imperative that we continue to check Iranian influence around the globe, and thwart future attacks.

Mr. KING. Well, I can't top that. Congratulations, Mr. Saab. Thank you.

Mr. SAAB. Thank you, very much.

Mr. KING. You are still coming here. Wow, okay.

Other Members of the subcommittee are reminded that opening statements may be submitted for the record.

[The statement of Ranking Member Thompson follows:]

STATEMENT OF RANKING MEMBER BENNIE G. THOMPSON

Iran poses one of the most complex foreign policy and National security challenges of the modern era. In 1984, the U.S. State Department listed Iran as a state sponsor of terrorism. According to the State Department, Iran provides funding, weapons, training, and sanctuary to numerous terrorist groups, most notably in Iraq, Afghanistan, and Lebanon, constituting a security concern to both the domestic and the international community.

According to experts, Hezbollah essentially still serves as a proxy military force for Iran. Hezbollah receives financial and material support from Iran and Syria, and its armed forces possess significant military and unconventional warfare capabilities that rival and in some cases exceed those of surrounding countries' armed forces and police. In addition to discussing Hezbollah today, I expect a comprehensive debate of the Joint Comprehensive Plan of Action, informally known as the Iran Nuclear Deal.

After thorough consideration, I supported the Iran Nuclear Deal. I recognize that like all multifaceted and varied agreements, there are drawbacks to the Iran Nuclear Deal. However, as I stated in September and continue to believe today, the deal will improve the security of our country and our allies and will curtail Iran's nuclear program. As a protective measure, some U.S. sanctions will remain in place under the deal.

The Nuclear Deal does not require the United States to suspend sanctions on Iran's support for terrorism, its human rights abuses, nor world-wide arms and WMD-related technology to Iran. Most importantly, the deal does not require the United States to remove or to reconsider Iran's designation as a state sponsor of terrorism, and all sanctions triggered by that designation will remain in place.

These provisions and the United States' refusal to negotiate them are proof that this remains a National security issue of utmost importance. Mistrust and tension between the governments of the United States and Iran has existed for decades and there have been periods of alliance and periods of contention. With the signing of the Iran Nuclear Deal, an examination of a way forward with Iran makes sense and is timely.

However, we should not submit to scare tactics or political grandstanding. Instead, we should ensure that this discussion is fact-based and accurate given our threat intelligence, not speculation, and focused on sensible solutions.

Mr. KING. We are pleased to have a distinguished panel of witnesses before us today on this vital topic.

The first witness will be Mr. Tzvi Kahn, who is a senior policy analyst for the Foreign Policy Initiative, where he has written extensively on Iran and their foreign and security policy. He previously served as the assistant director for policy and government affairs at AIPAC.

He holds a master's degree in Middle East Studies from the George Washington University's Elliott School of International Affairs and earned his bachelor's degree in English and in Classical Languages from Yeshiva University.

Mr. Kahn.

STATEMENT OF TZVI KAHN, SENIOR POLICY ANALYST, FOREIGN POLICY INITIATIVE

Mr. KAHN. Chairman King, Ranking Member Higgins, and distinguished Members of the subcommittee, thank you for the opportunity to testify this morning. In the post-Nuclear Deal era, Iran's long-standing objectives in the Middle East remain unchanged, regional hegemony and the contraction of U.S. forces and influence.

In fact, the Nuclear Deal makes these goals more achievable, since it provides Iran with billions of dollars in sanctions relief, which it will inevitably use to expand its global terror operations. President Obama has rightly stated that the United States can and must continue to fight Tehran's support for terrorism after the deal.

Such an effort, he said, would, in fact, be easier, now that the nuclear file has been closed. At the same time, he has also argued that the deal could ultimately lead to a broader rapprochement with Iran and strengthen moderate forces within the country.

Unfortunately, it has not turned out that way. In the 7 months since the deal, Tehran has continued and, in many respects, increased its regional aggression, its domestic repression, its violations of international laws and norms, and its open defiance of the United States and its allies.

In response, the administration has remained largely passive. The list of Iranian provocations is long and grim, but I will highlight just a few. In collaboration with Moscow, Tehran has increased its support for the bloody Assad regime. It backs the Lebanese terrorist group Hezbollah and Houthi.

It aids Shiite militias in Iraq that have killed more than 500 U.S. soldiers and that likely were responsible for kidnapping three Americans last month. It has tested ballistic missiles in violation of the U.N. Security Council resolutions.

It has test-fired rockets in dangerous proximity to a U.S. aircraft carrier. It has waged cyber attacks against the United States. It has captured U.S. soldiers and broadcast their surrender in an effort to humiliate America.

It has used U.S. prisoners as bargaining chips to secure the release of Iranian sanctions violators. It has carried out what the International Campaign for Human Rights in Iran calls the largest crackdown on human rights since the 2009 Green Revolution.

Why would Iran behave this way so soon after signing a landmark nuclear agreement with the international community? The reasons, I think, are both tactical and ideological. First, the deal has offered Iran a tactical opportunity to leverage it as a coercive mechanism in its dealings with Washington.

Recognizing that the preservation of the deal is the Obama administration's top foreign policy priority, Tehran has repeatedly threatened to walk away from it, if Washington punishes the regime for any kind of misbehavior.

In so doing, Tehran has deterred meaningful consequences for its actions. This ploy has proven quite successful. It has enabled Iran to set the terms of its relationship with America and to advance its extremist agenda with relative impunity.

Second, as multiple statements from Iran's Supreme Leader, Ayatollah Ali Khamenei, indicate, Tehran fears that the Nuclear Deal is in some way a ruse, aimed at advancing the Western effort to infiltrate its body politic, subvert its radical Islamist ideology, and ultimately overthrow the regime.

To be sure, Tehran's fears of Western infiltration date back to the Islamic Republic's founding in 1979 and are a key part of its conspiratorial world view, regardless of the reality.

But this time, its anxieties have an element of truth. After all, President Obama has repeatedly stated that a Nuclear Deal could help alter the fundamental nature of U.S.-Iranian relations.

For this reason, Iran has increased its aggression, in order to convey a simple message. In the post-Nuclear Deal era, Tehran's hostility towards the West will endure. There will be no rapprochement.

As the regime has repeatedly stated, the deal was purely transactional and had only one purpose: Sanctions relief. Thus, as a practical matter, the deal has not moderated Iran, but, in fact, has exacerbated its dangerous behavior.

What should the United States do? I believe that we need to make a fundamental paradigm shift in our relationship with Iran and adopt a comprehensive strategy, rooted in the premise that our policy on the Nuclear Deal and our policy on Iran's support for terrorism are inextricably linked.

How can the United States achieve this? By reestablishing deterrents and forcing Tehran to reassess the cost-benefit analysis of its behavior; by imposing meaningful new sanctions on Iran's Islamic Revolutionary Guard Corps, which spearheads Iran's regional aggression and domestic repression; by openly siding with our Gulf allies against Iran, in order to reduce its regional presence and influence; by treating Iran as part of the region's problems, especially Syria's Civil War, not as part of the solution.

In short, we need to reverse the current dynamic, so that it is Iran, not the United States, that fears the consequences of deliberate provocations. This process will not be easy, but if the United States continues its current path, I fear that Iranian aggression will likely continue to increase, further endangering our allies, our interests, and our National security.

Thank you, again, for the opportunity to testify today, and I look forward to your questions.

[The prepared statement of Mr. Kahn follows:]

PREPARED STATEMENT OF TZVI KAHN

FEBRUARY 11, 2016

Chairman King, Ranking Member Higgins, and distinguished Members of the subcommittee, thank you for the opportunity to testify before you this morning about the Iranian threat.

In this testimony, I analyze the impact of the July 2015 nuclear agreement, formally known as the Joint Comprehensive Plan of Action (JCPOA), on Iran's strategic decision making, regional and domestic ambitions, and policy toward the United States. I specifically attempt to explain why this agreement has failed to spur a rapprochement in U.S.-Iranian relations and instead exacerbated Tehran's hostility.

The JCPOA has not changed Iran's long-time objectives in the Middle East: Regional hegemony, the contraction of U.S. forces and influence, and the subjugation of Sunni Islamic states beneath a dominant Shiite crescent. The Nuclear Deal in fact makes these ends more achievable, since it provides Iran with billions of dollars in sanctions relief. Despite this opportunity, the leadership in Tehran fears that the JCPOA constitutes a ruse to infiltrate its body politic and moderate its radical Islamist ideology. As a result, Iran has increased its aggression against the United States and its allies in order to demonstrate that the Nuclear Deal will not alter its commitment to its vision of the Islamic Revolution.

As Tehran takes more destructive measures to demonstrate its Islamist bona fides, the JCPOA has also provided the Iranian regime with an opportunity to leverage the agreement as a bargaining chip in its dealings with Washington. Recognizing that the JCPOA's preservation amounts to the Obama administration's foremost foreign policy priority, Tehran has repeatedly threatened to withdraw from the deal in order to deter the United States from imposing any meaningful consequences for its aggression. This ploy has enabled the Islamist regime to set the terms of its relationship with America and advance its extremist agenda with relative impunity.

To reverse this dynamic, the United States must adopt a paradigm shift that treats Iran's nuclear program and non-nuclear aggression as interrelated problems that require a comprehensive strategy. It must seek to raise the costs of Tehran's belligerence by imposing meaningful penalties for any type of Iranian misbehavior—nuclear or non-nuclear. It should make clear not only that it does not consider Iran part of the solution to the region's problems, particularly Syria's civil war, but also that it actively opposes its rise as a regional power. The past 7 months of Iranian provocations already provide ample warning of Tehran's malign plans in the post-Nuclear Deal era. Now America must act to stop them.

AMERICA'S HOPE, IRAN'S SUSPICION

Over the past 2 years, the Obama administration has repeatedly portrayed a nuclear agreement as a means to achieve a broader U.S.-Iranian rapprochement that could spur Tehran's rise as a moderate regional power committed to peaceful coexistence with its Sunni neighbors.

In January 2014, President Obama suggested that a Nuclear Deal, in conjunction with other steps to stem Iran's extremist policies, could facilitate a new "equilibrium developing between Sunni, or predominantly Sunni, Gulf states and Iran in which there's competition, perhaps suspicion, but not an active or proxy warfare."[1] In March 2014, he advised America's Sunni Gulf allies to prepare for a new era in which the United States no longer favors the "existing order and the existing alignments" in the region, and has ceased to be "an implacable foe of Iran."[2]

"They've got a chance to get right with the world," said President Obama in December 2014, adding that Iran could become "a very successful regional power that was also abiding by international norms and international rules, and that would be good for everybody."[3] A nuclear agreement, he claimed in April 2015, may initiate a process that leads to a new "equilibrium in the region, and Sunni and Shia, Saudi and Iran start saying, 'Maybe we should lower tensions and focus on the extremists

[1] David Remnick, "Going the Distance," *The New Yorker*, January 27, 2014, *http://www.newyorker.com/magazine/2014/01/27/going-the-distance-david-remnick*.
[2] Jeffrey Goldberg, "Obama to Israel—Time Is Running Out," Bloomberg, March 2, 2014, *http://www.bloombergview.com/articles/2014-03-02/obama-to-israel-time-is-running-out*.
[3] Interview with Steve Inskeep, NPR, December 29, 2014, *http://www.npr.org/2014/12/29/372485968/transcript-president-obamas-full-npr-interview*.

like [ISIS] that would burn down this entire region if they could.'"[4] Moreover, he said that month, it may even "strengthen the hand of those more moderate forces inside of Iran."[5]

After Iran and the P5+1 finalized the JCPOA on July 14, 2015, the White House continued to press this line of argument. "They have the ability now to take some decisive steps to move toward a more constructive relationship with the world community," President Obama said that day. "And the truth of the matter," he added, "is that Iran will be and should be a regional power."[6] In August 2015, he cited Syria's civil war as a potential arena for cooperation, arguing that the deal held out the "the possibility that, having begun conversations around this narrow issue, that you start getting some broader discussions about Syria, for example."[7] On January 17, 2016, the JCPOA's Implementation Day, President Obama said the deal presented "the opportunity at least for Iran to work more cooperatively with nations around the world to advance their interests and the interests of people who are looking for peace and security for their families."[8]

For the Islamist regime, however, the negotiations constituted both an opportunity and a threat. On the one hand, it offered the prospect of long-sought sanctions relief that would restore Iran's ailing economy. On the other hand, as President Obama's own rhetoric seemed to indicate, an agreement could serve as a ruse to reorient Tehran's regional agenda and even temper its radical Islamist character, which Iran's supreme leader, Ayatollah Ali Khamenei, regards as the essence of the regime. Having achieved the former, Khamenei now aims to prevent the latter.

Tehran's fears of such U.S. ambitions long predate the international community's concern over Iran's nuclear program. At its root, Tehran's ideology, a product of the 1979 Islamic Revolution, views Shiite Iran as the vanguard of authentic Islam in a region corrupted by Western influence and values. Ayatollah Ruhollah Khomeini, the Islamic Republic's founding father and first supreme leader, argued that America poses not only a physical threat but also a spiritual threat: It seeks to destroy Islam and transform the Middle East into a secular, godless region marked by violence, greed, and promiscuity. In this conspiratorial worldview, both Israel and the Sunni Arab states are agents of the United States, which secretly guides and manipulates their actions as part of a nefarious plot to overthrow the Iranian regime. In this context, stated Khomeini, America's defeat constitutes not only a political goal, but also a religious imperative.[9]

These core principles of Iran's ideology remain unchanged, and lie at the heart of the Khamenei regime's identity. Waging war against the United States "is one of the principles of the [Islamic] Revolution," Khamenei said on August 4. "If fighting against arrogance does not take place, it means that we are not followers of the Holy Quran at all."[10] "The Revolution," he said on September 16, "is a permanent process, not a temporary one."[11] America, he said on October 7, "is a transgressor by nature. It is in the nature of world-devouring powers to transgress, to advance, to occupy and to dig-in their claws."[12] On August 17, he asserted that the United States "is the epitome of global arrogance" and "knows nothing about human morality and it is not ashamed of committing any crime—of any nature."[13] On November 3, he asserted—citing a statement by Ayatollah Khomeini—that America "was be-

[4] Thomas L. Friedman, "Iran and the Obama Doctrine," *The New York Times*, April 5, 2015, *http://www.nytimes.com/2015/04/06/opinion/thomas-friedman-the-obama-doctrine-and-iran-interview.html*.

[5] Interview with Steve Inskeep, NPR, April 7, 2015, *http://www.npr.org/templates/story/story.php?storyId=397933577*.

[6] Thomas L. Friedman, "Obama Makes His Case on Iran Nuclear Deal," *The New York Times*, July 14, 2015, *http://www.nytimes.com/2015/07/15/opinion/thomas-friedman-obama-makes-his-case-on-iran-nuclear-deal.html*.

[7] Interview with Fareed Zakaria, CNN, August 9, 2015, *http://transcripts.cnn.com/TRANSCRIPTS/1508/09/fzgps.01.html*.

[8] "Statement by the President on Iran," The White House, January 17, 2016, *https://www.whitehouse.gov/the-press-office/2016/01/17/statement-president-iran*.

[9] See Imam Khomeini, *Islam and Revolution: Writings and Declarations of Imam Khomeini* (1941–1980), Translated and Annotated by Hamid Algar (Mizan Press, 1981).

[10] "Leader's speech in meeting with students," Official website of Ayatollah Ali Khamenei, July 11, 2015, *http://english.khamenei.ir/news/2104/Leader-s-speech-in-meeting-with-students*.

[11] "IRGC blocks the enemy's infiltration," Official website of Ayatollah Ali Khamenei, September 16, 2015, *http://english.khamenei.ir/news/2155/IRGC-blocks-the-enemy-s-infiltration*.

[12] "Leader's speech in meeting with commanders and personnel of Islamic Revolution Guards Corps," Official website of Ayatollah Ali Khamenei, October 7, 2015, *http://english.khamenei.ir/news/2194/Leader-s-speech-in-meeting-with-commanders-and-personnel-of-Islamic*.

[13] "Leader's speech to members of Ahlul Bayt World Assembly and Islamic Radio and TV Union," Official website of Ayatollah Ali Khamenei, August 17, 2015, *http://english.khamenei.ir/news/2109/Leader-s-speech-to-members-of-Ahlul-Bayt-World-Assembly-and-Islamic*.

hind all problems" and lies at "the root of all evil things." "If they could destroy the Islamic Republic," Khamenei added, "they will not hesitate even for a moment."[14]

Similarly, he claimed on July 18, "the enemy planted the Zionist regime in the region so that they can create discord and busy regional countries with themselves."[15] On August 22, in an apparent reference to Sunni Arab nations opposed to Iran, he argued that the "enemies sometimes use certain Islamic countries to say and do what they want." These states, he continued, "have been deceived and used as a tool."[16] According to a November 4 statement on Khamenei's website, "Al-Qaeda, Al-Nusrah Front, FSA (Free Syrian Army), ISIS (Islamic State in Iraq and Syria) and many other names should not be confusing; they are all Western-backed mercenaries fighting proxy wars."[17] For Khamenei, the United States was even behind the November 2015 terror attacks in Paris that claimed 130 lives.[18]

Iran's ideology remains crucial to understanding Tehran's behavior in the post-Nuclear Deal era: Khameni fears that the Nuclear Deal, despite the opportunity it presents for economic recovery, represents yet another underhanded U.S. attempt to undermine the Islamic Revolution.

On October 7, he identified two types of negotiations: The modern type, which "means giving something and receiving something else in return," and the American type, which "means penetration."[19] "They pursue something called 'negotiations,'" he explained on September 9, "but negotiations are just an excuse and a tool for penetration. Negotiations are an instrument for imposing their demands."[20] On October 21, he contended that America entered the nuclear negotiations "not with the intention of resolving matters justly, but rather it was for the pursuit of their hostile goals against the Islamic Republic."[21] The United States, he noted on September 3, says the Nuclear Deal has provided it "with certain opportunities both inside Iran and in the region." However, he continued, "if they get close to these opportunities, this will be a starting point for nations and countries to become humiliated and backward and to experience various sufferings."[22]

To prevent such an outcome, Khamenei insisted during the talks that Iranian negotiators must focus exclusively on exchanging nuclear concessions for sanctions relief—that is, the "modern" type of negotiations—and would not prefigure any change in U.S.-Iranian relations, which could serve as an avenue for Western infiltration. Iran's sole "purpose of entering into the nuclear negotiations is to lift sanctions," he said on June 23, just 3 weeks before the JCPOA's finalization.[23] And by this standard, he declared after the deal, Tehran succeeded. "They wanted to use [the nuclear deal] as a means to exert influence in our country," he said on August 17, "but we blocked their path and we will definitely block their path in the future as well."[24]

---

[14] "'Death to America' means death to American policies and arrogance," Official website of Ayatollah Ali Khamenei, November 3, 2015, *http://english.khamenei.ir/news/2298/Death-to-America-means-death-to-American-policies-and-arrogance.*

[15] "Leader's speech in meeting with ambassadors of Islamic countries," Official website of Ayatollah Ali Khamenei, July 18, 2015, *http://english.khamenei.ir/news/2112/Leader-s-speech-in-meeting-with-ambassadors-of-Islamic-countries.*

[16] "Leader's speech to Hajj officials," Official website of Ayatollah Ali Khamenei, August 22, 2015, *http://english.khamenei.ir/news/2118/Leader-s-speech-to-Hajj-officials.*

[17] "ISIS qualifies for staging U.S.'s latest puppet show in the region," Official website of Ayatollah Ali Khamenei, November 4, 2015, *http://english.khamenei.ir/news/2164/ISIS-qualifies-for-staging-U-S-s-latest-puppet-show-in-the-region.*

[18] "Who is behind the Paris attacks?," Official website of Ayatollah Ali Khamenei video, 4:06, November 17, 2015, *http://english.khamenei.ir/news/2454/Who-is-behind-the-Paris-attacks.*

[19] "Leader's speech in meeting with commanders and personnel of Islamic Revolution Guards Corps," Official website of Ayatollah Ali Khamenei, October 7, 2015, *http://english.khamenei.ir/news/2194/Leader-s-speech-in-meeting-with-commanders-and-personnel-of-Islamic.*

[20] "Strong economy, developing science and revolutionary spirit," Official website of Ayatollah Ali Khamenei, September 9, 2015, *http://english.khamenei.ir/news/2136/Strong-economy-developing-science-and-revolutionary-spirit.*

[21] "Leader's letter to President Rouhani regarding the JCPOA," Official website of Ayatollah Ali Khamenei, October 21, 2015, *http://english.khamenei.ir/news/2336/Leader-s-letter-to-President-Rouhani-regarding-the-JCPOA.*

[22] "Leader's speech in meeting with Assembly of Experts," Official website of Ayatollah Ali Khamenei, September 3, 2015, *http://english.khamenei.ir/news/2132/Leader-s-speech-in-meeting-with-Assembly-of-Experts.*

[23] "Leader's speech in meeting with government officials," Official website of Ayatollah Ali Khamenei, June 23, 2015, *http://english.khamenei.ir/news/2088/Leader-s-speech-in-meeting-with-government-officials.*

[24] "Leader's speech to members of Ahlul Bayt World Assembly and Islamic Radio and TV Union," Official website of Ayatollah Ali Khamenei, August 17, 2015, *http://english.khamenei.ir/news/2109/Leader-s-speech-to-members-of-Ahlul-Bayt-World-Assembly-and-Islamic.*

On September 9, he again asserted triumphantly that Tehran "did not allow [nego-tiators] to negotiate with America on other matters."[25]

Thus, according to the supreme leader, the Nuclear Deal marked not a precursor to further cooperation, but an "exceptional" case—as Khamenei put it on July 18—of U.S.-Iranian diplomacy that served only to advance Tehran's narrowly-defined economic goals. "Our policy towards the arrogant government of America will not change in any way despite these negotiations and the document that has been pre-pared," he stressed that day. "As we have said many times, we have no negotiations with America on different global and regional issues . . . The American policies in the region are 180 degrees the opposite of the policies of the Islamic Republic."[26]

At the same time, however, Khamenei recognized that the Obama administra-tion's intense yearning for an agreement also presented Iran with an invaluable strategic opportunity: By repeatedly threatening to withdraw from the agreement if the United States attempted to punish the regime for its support of terrorism, Tehran could use the JCPOA as a coercive mechanism to deter meaningful con-sequences for its misbehavior, both with respect to the nuclear file and with respect to the broader region. Ironically, the JCPOA could actually facilitate Iran's regional aggression rather than spur the regime to discontinue it for the sake of a U.S. rap-prochement.

SEVEN MONTHS OF PROVOCATIONS

The diplomatic relationship between the United States and Iran in the post-Nu-clear Deal era reflects the asymmetry of the Nuclear Deal itself. In its eagerness to reach an agreement, the United States abdicated virtually every red line it had publicly articulated during the negotiations—from dismantling Iran's nuclear infra-structure and ensuring anytime-anywhere inspections to linking sanctions relief with sustained compliance.[27] Today, in its eagerness to preserve the agreement, the administration has failed to offer a meaningful challenge to Iran's regional aggres-sion, domestic repression, violations of international laws and norms, and other acts of defiance against the United States and its interests.

This imbalance has created a dynamic that allows Tehran to set the terms of U.S.-Iran diplomacy. Whereas the White House has exerted great pains to avoid al-most any step that Tehran may perceive as hostile, the Islamist regime has felt free to refrain from exercising any reciprocal discretion. In so doing, it has ruthlessly ex-ploited Washington's desperation to safeguard the JCPOA.

Regional Aggression

Since July 2015, Iran, in conjunction with Russia, has strengthened its military support for Damascus, thereby prolonging and exacerbating Syria's bloody civil war. For Tehran, the preservation of the Assad regime, its foremost regional client, con-stitutes its single greatest regional priority. A pro-Iran regime in Syria gives Tehran a foothold in the Levant and provides a pathway for military and financial support of its Lebanese proxy, the terrorist group Hezbollah, which has also benefited from increased Iranian largesse since the JCPOA.[28] According to Staffan de Mistura, the U.N. special envoy for Syria, Iran spends $6 billion annually to prop up Assad's re-gime.[29]

On July 18, Supreme Leader Khamenei explicitly affirmed that the deal would not affect Iran's support for Damascus. "In Syria," he said, "the policy of arrogance is to overthrow—at any price—the government that is known for its resistance against Zionism, but our policy is against theirs."[30] In the coming months, fearing that any dispute with Tehran would prompt it to abandon the JCPOA, the Obama administration reversed its earlier position that Assad must leave power as part of

[25] "Strong economy, developing science and revolutionary spirit," Official website of Ayatollah Ali Khamenei, September 9, 2015, *http://english.khamenei.ir/news/2136/Strong-economy-de-veloping-science-and-revolutionary-spirit.*

[26] "Leader's sermons at Eid ul-Fitr prayers," Official website of Ayatollah Ali Khamenei, July 18, 2015, *http://english.khamenei.ir/news/2102/Leader-s-sermons-at-Eid-ul-Fitr-prayers.*

[27] See Tzvi Kahn, "FPI Analysis: What U.S. Officials Required, What the Iran Deal Concedes," Foreign Policy Initiative, July 28, 2015, *http://www.foreignpolicyi.org/content/fpi-analysis-what-us-officials-required-what-iran-deal-concedes.*

[28] See Max Peck, *Doubling Down on Damascus: Iran's Military Surge to Save the Assad Re-gime*, Foundation for Defense of Democracies, January 2016, *http://www.defenddemocracy.org/content/uploads/documents/Doubling_Down_on_Damascus.pdf.*

[29] Eli Lake, "Iran Spends Billions to Prop Up Assad," Bloomberg, June 9, 2015, *http://www.bloombergview.com/articles/2015-06-09/iran-spends-billions-to-prop-up-assad.*

[30] "Leader's speech in meeting with ambassadors of Islamic countries," Official website of Aya-tollah Ali Khamenei, July 18, 2015, *http://english.khamenei.ir/news/2112/Leader-s-speech-in-meeting-with-ambassadors-of-Islamic-countries.*

a negotiated resolution, effectively putting Washington on the same page as Tehran.[31]

At the same time, Iran has also continued to support its other proxies and foment violence throughout the Middle East. In Iraq, Shiite militias remain the beneficiaries of robust Iranian military and economic aid, and likely were responsible for kidnapping 3 Americans in Baghdad last month.[32] In Afghanistan, Iran has recruited thousands of Afghans, some by force, to fight in Syria, Human Rights Watch stated in January,[33] while General John Campbell, commander of U.S. forces in Afghanistan, said in October 2015 that he has received reports of Iranian money and arms flowing to the Taliban.[34]

In Bahrain, the government arrested 47 members of an Iran-backed terror cell that it accused of planning attacks in the country,[35] while in late September 2015, the Gulf island state withdrew its ambassador from Iran after the discovery of a large bomb-making factory linked to Tehran's Islamic Revolutionary Guard Corps (IRGC).[37] In Yemen, Iran continues to train and equip the Houthis. In September 2015, Saudi Arabia intercepted an Iranian ship in the Arabian Sea carrying missile launchers, anti-tank shells and missiles destined for the Tehran-backed rebels.[37]

Nuclear and Ballistic Missile Defiance

Since the JCPOA's finalization, Tehran has openly defied the United States and international community on key disclosure provisions related to inspections of Iran's nuclear program. Under the agreement, Iran committed to resolving the international community's outstanding concerns about the possible military dimensions (PMD) of its nuclear program. Instead, it stonewalled the International Atomic Energy Agency's (IAEA) investigation, providing misleading or incomplete responses to the U.N. watchdog's questions. The agency ultimately concluded that Iran concealed, and continues to conceal, efforts to weaponize nuclear material, and engaged in weapons-related work as recently as 2009.[38] Nevertheless, the United States voted in favor of an IAEA Board of Governors resolution that closed the PMD file,[39] paving the way for the JCPOA's implementation and directly contradicting the Obama administration's earlier pledge to seek full PMD disclosure as part of a final deal.[40]

Similarly, Iran has stated that it will refuse to allow inspectors to enter any military sites,[41] effectively repudiating President Obama's claim that the JCPOA allows the IAEA "to access any suspicious location."[42] With the consent of the United States, Tehran also reached a confidential side deal with the IAEA that permits it to self-inspect the Parchin military complex, making a further mockery of the verification regime.[43] Olli Heinonen, former deputy director general and head of

[31] Matthew Lee and Bradley Klapper, "Assad can stay, for now: Kerry accepts Russian stance," Associated Press, December 15, 2015, *http://bigstory.ap.org/article/ed88e4c5d57341eba365a966300f67e3/kerry-moscow-talks-syria-ukraine*.

[32] "2 groups eyed in kidnapping of Americans in Baghdad," CBS News, January 21, 2016, *http://www.cbsnews.com/news/iraq-shiite-militias-eyed-kidnapping-americans-dora-baghdad*.

[33] "Iran Sending Thousands of Afghans to Fight in Syria," Human Rights Watch, January 29, 2016, *https://www.hrw.org/news/2016/01/29/iran-sending-thousands-afghans-fight-syria*.

[34] General John Campbell, "Gen. Campbell Confirms There are Reports that Iran is Arming the Taliban," YouTube video, 0:54, posted by Senator Ayotte, October 6, 2015; see also Margherita Stancati, "Iran Backs Taliban With Cash and Arms," *The Wall Street Journal*, June 11, 2015, *http://www.wsj.com/articles/iran-backs-taliban-with-cash-and-arms-1434065528*.

[35] "Bahrain says foils plans for attack by Iran-linked terrorist group," Reuters, November 4, 2015, *http://www.reuters.com/article/us-bahrain-iran-idUSKCN0ST2GJ20151104*.

[36] "Bahrain withdraws ambassador from Iran after bomb-factory find," Reuters, October 1, 2015, *http://www.reuters.com/article/us-bahrain-security-iran-idUSKCN0RV5E620151001*.

[37] Ahmed Al Omran and Asa Fitch, "Saudi Coalition Seizes Iranian Boat Carrying Weapons to Yemen," *The Wall Street Journal*, September 30, 2015, *http://www.wsj.com/articles/saudi-coalition-seizes-iranian-boat-carrying-weapons-to-rebels-in-yemen-1443606304*.

[38] IAEA Board of Governors, *Final Assessment on Past and Present Outstanding Issues regarding Iran's Nuclear Programme* (GOV/2015/68), December 2, 2015, *https://www.iaea.org/sites/default/files/gov-2015-68.pdf*.

[39] Francois Murphy and Shadia Nasralla, "U.N. watchdog decides to close nuclear weapons probe of Iran," Reuters, December 15, 2015, *http://www.reuters.com/article/us-nuclear-iran-resolution-idUSKBN0TY1YF20151215*.

[40] Interview with Judy Woodruff, PBS Newshour, April 8, 2015, *http://www.pbs.org/newshour/bb/iran-must-disclose-past-nuclear-military-activities-final-deal-says-kerry*.

[41] Mohammad Javad Zarif, Interview with Christiane Amanpour, CNN, July 14, 2015, *http://www.cnn.com/TRANSCRIPTS/1507/14/ampr.01.html*.

[42] "Statement by the President on Iran," The White House, July 14, 2015, *https://www.whitehouse.gov/the-press-office/2015/07/14/statement-president-iran*.

[43] "Text of draft agreement between IAEA, Iran," Associated Press, August 20, 2015, *http://news.yahoo.com/text-draft-agreement-between-iaea-iran-193603978.html*.

safeguards at the IAEA, stated that the procedures at Parchin "departed significantly from well-established and proven safeguards practices." Moreover, he said, the P5+1's failure to object to Iran's clean-up efforts at the site after the IAEA had requested access effectively "acquiesces to Iran's violations of the spirit, if not the letter, of international inspections standards."[44]

In October and November, Iran conducted two ballistic missile tests, directly violating a U.N. Security Council resolution that prohibits such actions.[45] On January 17, the United States belatedly announced new designations of an illicit procurement network supporting Iran's ballistic missile programs,[46] a move it had previously postponed reportedly in order to facilitate a prisoner swap between the two nations (see next section).[47] Nevertheless, in light of the billions of dollars in sanctions relief Iran received as part of Implementation Day, the new sanctions amounted to pinpricks, prompting an unrepentant Tehran to respond that it will now continue its ballistic missile program "more seriously."[48]

American Hostages as Bargaining Chips

While the safe return of U.S. hostages from Iran's notorious prisons should elicit relief, the recent prisoner swap between Washington and Tehran comes at a price that ultimately serves to encourage future Iranian belligerence. In exchange for innocent Americans incarcerated on trumped-up charges, including *Washington Post* reporter Jason Rezaian, U.S. Marine veteran Amir Hekmati, Idaho pastor Saeed Abedini, and previously undisclosed prisoner Nosratollah Khosravi-Roodsari, the Obama administration released seven Iranians who violated sanctions on Tehran's nuclear or military program. (Iran released another previously undisclosed prisoner, Matthew Trevithick, separately.) The White House also dismissed charges against 14 other Iranians it had sought to arrest.

Such a trade hardly constitutes a "reciprocal humanitarian gesture," as President Obama claimed.[49] In fact, the swap effectively incentivizes Iran to capture more U.S. hostages in order to engage in further extortion. Tehran already probably recognizes such potential: The exchange notably failed to secure the release of another prisoner, Siamak Namazi, whom Iran likely retained to serve as a future bargaining chip for concessions it failed to obtain as part of it. Moreover, the United States acquired no new information about the location of former FBI agent Robert Levinson, who went missing in Iran in 2007 and may be languishing in an Iranian prison.

Equally troubling, the 14 pardoned Iranians included two men who helped transfer soldiers and weapons to the Assad regime and Hezbollah, thereby serving to enflame and prolong Syria's bloody civil war. Hamid Arabnejad and Gholamreza Mahmoudi, senior officials at Iran's privately-owned Mahan Air, have long utilized the airline to transfer soldiers and arms to the Syrian battlefield—and may now continue their efforts with impunity.[50]

Moreover, if the Obama administration delayed the announcement of ballistic missile sanctions over concerns it would it would torpedo the prisoner exchange, Iran may have learned an even more troubling lesson: Additional hostages can prevent new sanctions.

Naval Aggression

Iran's capture of 10 U.S. Navy sailors in the Persian Gulf on January 13—just hours before President Obama's 2016 State of the Union address and days before Implementation Day—marked yet another attempt to demonstrate that Iran's hostility toward America would endure in the post-Nuclear Deal era. In fact, the re-

[44] Olli Heinonen, "Strengthening the Verification and Implementation of the Joint Comprehensive Plan of Action," Foundation for Defense of Democracies, November 2015, *http://www.defenddemocracy.org/content/uploads/documents/Strengthening_Verification_JCPOA.-pdf*.

[45] Jay Solomon and Gordon Lubold, "Iran Test-Fires Another Missile, U.S. Says," *The Wall Street Journal*, December 8, 2015, *http://www.wsj.com/articles/white-house-backs-closing-u-n-probe-into-irans-nuclear-program-1449595905*.

[46] "Treasury Sanctions Those Involved in Ballistic Missile Procurement for Iran," U.S. Department of the Treasury, January 17, 2016, *https://www.treasury.gov/press-center/press-releases/Pages/jl0322.aspx*.

[47] Lesley Wroughton, Patricia Zengerle, and Matt Spetalnick, "Exclusive: In negotiating to free Americans in Iran, U.S. blinked on new sanctions," Reuters, January 16, 2015, *http://www.reuters.com/article/us-iran-nuclear-prisoners-exclusive-idUSKCN0UU0WS*.

[48] "Iran Vows to Continue Advancing Missile Program," Fars News Agency, January 18, 2016, *http://en.farsnews.com/newstext.aspx?nn=13941028000442*.

[49] "Statement by the President on Iran," The White House, January 17, 2016, *https://www.whitehouse.gov/the-press-office/2016/01/17/statement-president-iran*.

[50] Josh Rogin, "Prisoner Swap May Help Iran Arm Assad," Bloomberg, January 17, 2016, *http://www.bloombergview.com/articles/2016-01-17/prisoner-swap-may-help-iran-arm-assad*.

gime's release of video footage of the sailors' surrender, as well as a video of one sailor issuing an apology, not only reflected a deliberate effort to humiliate the United States, but may have violated international law. Still, rather than penalize Iran for this aggression, Secretary of State John Kerry thanked Tehran for its "cooperation in swiftly resolving" the crisis it had created.[51]

The incident, said Maj. Gen. Hassan Firouzabadi, chair of Iran's Armed Forces General Staff, "demonstrated the awareness and precision of the Iranian armed forces regarding American movements in the region. It taught them how vulnerable they are against the Islamic Republic's mighty forces."[52] Brig. Gen. Hossein Salami, deputy commander of the IRGC, expressed similar sentiments. "No country in the world has been able to detain an American soldier since World War II," he gloated. "Yet when these soldiers entered our waters, small Iranian vessels . . . surrounded and arrested them. These 10 sailors surrendered to 5 or 6 young IRGC members."[53] At the end of January, Supreme Leader Khamenei awarded medals of honor to the IRGC commanders involved in the seizure.[54]

The episode followed a similar act of Iranian naval aggression less than 3 weeks earlier. On December 26, Iran test-fired rockets near the USS Harry S. Truman, an American aircraft carrier, almost triggering an international crisis.[55] "These actions were highly provocative, unsafe, and unprofessional and call into question Iran's commitment to the security of a waterway vital to international commerce," said Navy Commander Kyle Raines, spokesman for the U.S. Central Command.[56] Nevertheless, the United States apparently did nothing in response.

Domestic Oppression

Iranian human rights abuses have increased dramatically since the JCPOA. In fact, according to the International Campaign for Human Rights in Iran, Tehran in late 2015 carried out the "largest [human rights] crackdown since the violent state suppression of the protests that followed the disputed 2009 presidential election in Iran."[57] In recent weeks, the regime has also moved to disqualify thousands of reformist candidates from running in Iran's upcoming parliamentary elections.[58] The new repression comes as a direct response to the JCPOA: Tehran seeks to reinforce its message that a post-Nuclear Deal Iran will continue to oppose democratic forces that appear to embrace Western values of liberty and equality.

In October 2015, Dr. Ahmed Shaheed, the United Nations' special rapporteur on the situation of human rights in Iran, released a report detailing a grim litany of human rights abuses over the past year.[59] Perhaps most notably, the document states that Iran continues "to execute more individuals per capita than any other country in the world." Moreover, it noted, Iran has tortured prisoners and denied them access to lawyers; restricted the political rights of religious minorities and regime opponents; curbed women's rights in civil, political, social, and economic arenas; and persecuted Baha'is, Christians, and Sufi Dervish minorities. At the same time, Tehran has continued to reject continuous requests—issued in vain by the office of the special rapporteur since 2005—for country visits.

The report nonetheless expressed hope that the nuclear agreement will spur the regime "to redouble its efforts" to improve human rights. The data it catalogues, however, suggest that such a prospect remains unduly optimistic. In fact, in an

---

[51] "On U.S. Navy Sailors' Departure From Iran," U.S. Department of State," January 13, 2016, *http://www.state.gov/secretary/remarks/2016/01/251139.htm*.

[52] Sepah News, January 13, 2016. Translated by American Enterprise Institute Critical Threats Project, "Iran News Round Up," January 13, 2016, *http://www.irantracker.org/iran-news-round-january-13-2016*.

[53] Defa Press, January 15, 2016. Translated by American Enterprise Institute Critical Threats Project, "Iran News Round Up," January 15, 2016, *http://www.irantracker.org/iran-news-round-january-15-2016*.

[54] "Iran leader awards medals to IRGC commanders," Press TV, January 31, 2016, *http://www.presstv.ir/Detail/2016/01/31/448139/Iran-leader-awards-medals-to-IRGC-commanders*.

[55] Jim Miklaszewski, Courtney Kube, Ali Arouzi and Alastair Jamieson, "U.S. Carrier Harry S. Truman Has Close Call With Iranian Rockets," NBC News, December 30, 2015, *http://www.nbcnews.com/news/world/u-s-carrier-harry-s-truman-has-close-call-iranian-n487536*.

[56] "Iranian Revolutionary Guards fired rockets near U.S. warships in Gulf-U.S.," Reuters, December 29, 2015, *http://www.reuters.com/article/usa-iran-warship-idUSKBN0UD00R20151230*.

[57] "Largest Wave of Arrests by Iran's Revolutionary Guards Since 2009," International Campaign for Human Rights in Iran, November 19, 2015, *https://www.iranhumanrights.org/2015/11/irgc-intelligence-arrests*.

[58] Aresu Eqbali and Asa Fitch, "Iran Hard-Liners Reassert Influence on Election Slate," *The Wall Street Journal*, January 19, 2016, *http://www.wsj.com/articles/iran-hard-liners-reassert-influence-on-election-slate-1453227140*.

[59] U.N. General Assembly, 70th Session, *Situation of human rights in the Islamic Republic of Iran* (A/70/411), October 6, 2015, *http://shaheedoniran.org/wp-content/uploads/2015/10/SR-Report-Iran-Oct2015.pdf*.

irony fraught with bleak symbolism, the Islamist regime—as the International Campaign for Human Rights in Iran recently observed—has even attempted to silence Iranian media outlets critical of the JCPOA.[60]

NEEDED: A PARADIGM SHIFT

On a practical level, Iran has continued provoking the United States in the post-Nuclear Deal era for a simple reason: Because it can. By making clear that it values the preservation of the JCPOA above all else, the Obama administration has effectively enabled Tehran to use the agreement as a bargaining chip to secure its broader agenda. Put differently, the JCPOA offers Tehran the tactical means to advance its ideological commitment to the defeat of America's efforts to moderate the regime. In this sense, the JCPOA has effectively backfired on the White House, serving to undermine rather than facilitate President Obama's stated goals for a post-Nuclear Deal rapprochement.

To be sure, Iran has complied with the core initial requirements of the Nuclear Deal: It has reduced its stockpile of low-enriched uranium by 98 percent, removed the core of the Arak heavy water reactor, and disabled 12,000 centrifuges. These developments, however, should offer little comfort. Tehran possessed strong incentives to comply with the JCPOA's preliminary obligations: Reentry into the global economy and restored access to as much as $100 billion in frozen assets. But now that the regime has achieved these goals, it retains fewer incentives to keep its commitments in the long term. In fact, Iran can now simply engage in smaller-scale violations of the JCPOA but simultaneously deter any meaningful penalty by threatening to abandon the agreement in its entirety. In effect, it can challenge the White House to choose between punishing minor violations, thereby giving Iran cover to abandon the JCPOA, or allowing the deal to dissolve over time through the sheer accumulation of Iranian infringements.

The regime's preference for modest, incremental cheating would be consistent with its decades-long history of flouting nuclear agreements: As Mark Dubowitz of the Foundation for Defense of Democracies has observed, "The Iranian regime cheats incrementally, not egregiously, even though the sum total of its incremental cheating is egregious."[61] Perhaps more notably, it may explain why the JCPOA, likely at Iran's insistence, contains no provision for addressing incremental cheating, and allows snapback sanctions only in the event of vaguely defined "significant non-performance."[62] Ambiguous statements from the Obama administration that the United States possesses a "host of calibrated penalty tools" to address minor violations are unlikely to impress Ayatollah Khamenei.[63]

Moreover, American inaction can cause other States in the region to freelance their own efforts to combat Tehran, often at the expense of U.S. interests and values. The recent contretemps between Saudi Arabia and Iran, triggered by Riyadh's unjust execution of a pro-Iran Shiite cleric, reflects the inevitable result of a U.S. policy that remains willing to sacrifice regional stability on the altar of the Nuclear Deal. By treating Iran as a regional partner, America may risk unintended consequences that serve to enflame tensions between Iran and countries that still treat the Islamic Republic as their enemy. If America's Sunni allies lack faith in America's willingness to defend them against an increasingly aggressive Tehran, they may accelerate their own pursuit of nuclear weapons, thereby heightening proliferation concerns.

So long as the Obama administration fails to appreciate the nature and implications of Tehran's strategy and objectives, the Islamist regime's aggression will continue to intensify in the months and years to come. To reverse this dynamic, the United States must adopt a fundamental paradigm shift in its approach to its relationship with Tehran. Rather than treat Iran's nuclear program and Iran's non-nuclear belligerence as separate problems, Washington should aim to address them both as part of a comprehensive strategy rooted in the premise that Iran's fear of Western infiltration continues to guide its view of the Nuclear Deal.

---

[60] "Rouhani Government Suppresses Nuclear Deal's Critics," International Campaign for Human Rights in Iran, August 5, 2015, *https://www.iranhumanrights.org/2015/08/publication-shutdown*.

[61] "The Iran Nuclear Deal and its Impact on Terrorism Financing," Testimony before the House Financial Services Committee, July 22, 2015, *http://financialservices.house.gov/uploadedfiles/hhrg-114-ba00-wstate-mdubowitz-20150722.pdf*.

[62] Joint Comprehensive Plan of Action, July 14, 2015, Paragraph 36, *https://assets.documentcloud.org/documents/2165399/full-text-of-the-iran-nuclear-deal.pdf*.

[63] Adam Szubin, "Beyond the Vote: Implications for the Sanctions Regime on Iran," Keynote Address before The Washington Institute for Near East Policy, September 16, 2015, *http://www.washingtoninstitute.org/uploads/Documents/other/SzubinTranscript20150916-v2.pdf*.

In practice, this means that the United States must seek to raise the costs to Iran for its on-going regional aggression by increasing terrorism-related sanctions and taking steps to deter international investment in entities affiliated with the IRGC, which spearheads Iran's global terror operations and bears responsibility for many of its human rights abuses.[64] It means that the United States must impose meaningful punishments for *any* violation—major or minor—of the JCPOA or U.N. Security Council resolutions. It means that the United States must partner with Sunni Arab states opposed to Iran, including Saudi Arabia, notwithstanding other policy disagreements. And finally, it means that the White House cannot continue to treat Iran as a potential partner in solving the region's problems, particularly Syria's civil war.

Such an approach would represent a dramatic reversal of President Obama's original hopes for U.S.-Iranian relations after the Nuclear Deal. Nevertheless, a robust defense of U.S. allies and National interests offers the best prospect for actually effecting meaningful Iranian change in the long term. Iran will not modify its policies in response to American goodwill, but in response to deterrent steps that seek to alter Tehran's cost-benefit analysis. If the White House continues to hope, against overwhelming evidence, that Iran will reciprocate America's goodwill gestures on its own accord, it should not be surprised if Iran concludes that it has little to lose by continuing to provoke the United States.

Thank you again for the opportunity to testify today. I look forward to your questions.

Mr. KING. Thank you, Mr. Kahn.

Our next witness is Mr. Ilan Berman. He is vice president of the American Foreign Policy Council in Washington, DC, and is an acknowledged expert on regional security in the Middle East, Central Asia, and the Russian Federation, and has consulted for both the U.S. Central Intelligence Agency and the Department of Defense.

Mr. Berman is a member of the associated faculty at Missouri State University's Department of Defense and Strategic Studies, and serves as a columnist for Forbes.com and *The Washington Times,* and is the editor of the *Journal of International Security Affairs.* He has written several books, including the most recent, "Iran's Strategic Penetration of Latin America," published in 2014.

Recognized for 5 minutes. Thank you, Mr. Berman.

Mr. BERMAN. Thank you.

Mr. KING. When I say 5 minutes, just keep it roughly within that time. Don't worry about it.

STATEMENT OF ILAN BERMAN, VICE PRESIDENT, AMERICAN FOREIGN POLICY COUNCIL

Mr. BERMAN. Okay. Thank you, Mr. Chairman. Thank you, and thank you Ranking Member Higgins, and distinguished Members of the subcommittee. It is an honor to appear here today to discuss a topic that I think is of the utmost strategic importance to the United States, that is, Iran's sponsorship of terrorism and how it is going to be affected by the new Nuclear Deal, formerly known as the Joint Comprehensive Plan of Action.

I think it is fair to say, just as an opening statement, that, although the White House has argued that the Nuclear Deal closes the book on the Iranian nuclear file, it actually opens the book on a new and more challenging phase of U.S. Middle East policy.

---

[64] See Emanuele Ottolenghi, "The Iran Nuclear Deal and its Impact on Iran's Islamic Revolutionary Guards Corps," Testimony before the House Committee on Foreign Affairs's Subcommittee on the Middle East and North Africa, September 17, 2015, *http://www.defenddemocracy.org/content/uploads/documents/Ottolenghi_HFAC_IranDeal_IRGC.-pdf.*

It does so for at least 3 reasons. First, the JCPOA does not dismantle Iran's nuclear capability. In fact, it does the opposite. There are key provisions in the agreement, in particular in the annexes of the agreement, that commit the P5+1 countries to strengthening and reinforcing Iran's nuclear infrastructure and processes over the next decade.

The end result is an Iranian nuclear program that is slower, but one that is ultimately stronger. The second flaw with the JCPOA is that the agreement actually encourages further proliferation. It does not close off all of the pathways by which Iran can acquire nuclear capability. It focuses solely, or overwhelmingly, on domestic indigenous development of such a capability.

Almost entirely unaddressed by the terms of the JCPOA is the parallel pathway of clandestine acquisition of nuclear capabilities from abroad, a relationship that Iran can activate with such actors as North Korea or private entities in China.

But most significant of all is the fact that the JCPOA provides Iran with what amounts to an enormous economic windfall. As part of the terms of the JCPOA, the P5+1 countries agreed to release to Iran upwards of $100 billion in previously escrowed oil revenue.

Today, in the aftermath of implementation day, in mid-January, Iran has full, unencumbered access to these funds. The scope of this stimulus is truly enormous. It amounts to roughly a quarter of Iran's annual GDP, which totaled $415 billion in 2014.

The proportional impact would be as if the United States received an economic infusion of roughly $4.2 trillion over the near term. The magnitude of this is likely to empower a range of destructive Iranian behaviors in the years ahead, ranging from military modernization plans, which have been already articulated by the regime, to greater Iranian support for rogue regime partners, such as Venezuela, Bolivia, and Ecuador.

Most important of all is that it actually permits Iran to expand significantly its investments in the support of international terrorism. According to the Congressional Research Service, Iran currently spends between $3.5 billion and $16 billion a year on the support of terrorism, ranging from Hezbollah and Hamas and the Palestinian Islamic Jihad, to the Syrian regime, to Yemen's Houthi rebels, to Iraq's Shiite militias.

If just one-tenth of the new-found economic stimulus inherent in the JCPOA is used in this arena, it would effectively double or even triple Iran's investment in global terrorism. In the context of the U.S. homeland, I think this plays out in two principal arenas.

The first is Latin America, where, over the last decade, Iran has systematically expanded both its formal contacts with the region's regimes and its informal strategic presence. The late Argentine prosecutor, Alberto Nisman, detailed in 2013 that over the last 3 decades, Iran has built an extensive network of intelligence bases and covert centers in no fewer than 8 countries.

This is the network that empowered the 1994 bombing of the AMIA Jewish cultural center in Buenos Aires, and it is also the one that allowed Iran to either instigate or support 3 separate plots targeting the U.S. homeland in the last decade.

The 2007 plot to blow up the fuel tanks underneath the JFK International Airport, the October 2011 attempt to assassinate

Saudi Arabia's ambassador to the United States here in Washington, and a plot by Venezuelan and Iranian diplomats to conduct cyber-attacks on U.S. defense and civilian infrastructure.

The presence of Hezbollah has grown similarly. Over the last several years, a string of incidents, ranging from the apprehension of Hezbollah operatives in Peru, to revelations about Venezuelan official assistance, to Hezbollah operatives in the provision of state-supported passports, demonstrate that Hezbollah has both the mobility and the capability to post a significant threat.

The risks for American security in this context are both clear and present. As Iran begins to enrich itself, as a result of the JCPOA, we can expect more activity in this arena. For the purposes of time, the second arena where Iran is significantly likely to expand its activities in the U.S. homeland, and that is cyber space, I will leave to the questions, if you have any.

But let me conclude by saying that now that the implementation of the JCPOA has begun, Iran's ability to carry out a range of rogue behaviors has expanded exponentially. It is incumbent upon all of us, and upon the U.S. Congress, to watch what Iran is going, not only in the theaters where it is active currently, primarily in the Middle East, in Syria, but also in theaters further afield, because Iran's global ambition is truly global. Iran's global ambition is now much more fully funded, as a result of the Nuclear Deal.

Thank you.

[The prepared statement of Mr. Berman follows:]

PREPARED STATEMENT OF ILAN BERMAN

FEBRUARY 11, 2016

Chairman King, Ranking Member Higgins, distinguished Members of the subcommittee: It is an honor to appear before you today to discuss Iran's on-going sponsorship of international terrorism and the impact that the new Nuclear Deal, formally known as the Joint Comprehensive Plan of Action (JCPOA), will have upon it. It is a topic that is of critical importance to the security of the United States and our allies abroad. While the Obama administration has argued that the signing of the JCPOA has enhanced both U.S. and global security, there is compelling evidence to the contrary: Namely, that the passage of the agreement has ushered in a new and more challenging phase in U.S. Mideast policy.

SHORTFALLS OF THE JCPOA

While the JCPOA can be said to include some beneficial elements—including short-term constraints on Iranian uranium enrichment, a reduction in the number of centrifuges operated by the Islamic Republic, and a delay of the "plutonium track" of the regime's nuclear program—there is broad consensus among National security practitioners, military experts, scientists, and analysts that the agreement is woefully deficient in several respects.

First, the new Nuclear Deal does not dismantle Iran's nuclear capability, as originally envisioned by the United States and its negotiating partners. Contrary to the White House's pledges at the outset of talks between Iran and the P5+1 nations in November 2013, the JCPOA does not irrevocably reduce Iran's nuclear potential. In fact, it does the opposite; under key provisions of the JCPOA (specifically, those contained in Annex I, III, and IV of the agreement),[1] the P5+1 nations have committed themselves to strengthening and reinforcing Iran's nuclear infrastructure and processes over the next 10 years. As a result, the JCPOA enables a slower—but ultimately a stronger—Iranian nuclear program. When the agreement expires a decade

---

[1] Annex I, Section H codifies Russia's commitment to cooperate with Iran on nuclear research at the Fordow Fuel Enrichment Plant. Annex III, Section D enshrines a European commitment to aid Iran in strengthening its nuclear security. Under Annex IV, Section 2, the P5+1 powers pledge to provide international assistance to Iran in mastering the nuclear fuel cycle through fuel fabrication.

from now, the Islamic Republic will be much closer to a breakout capability than it is today.

The new Nuclear Deal likewise incentivizes further proliferation, both on the part of Iran and by its neighbors. Although President Obama has claimed that the JCPOA closes off "all" of the pathways by which Iran can acquire a nuclear capability,[2] it focuses overwhelmingly on Iran's indigenous development—its domestic facilities, stockpiles, and nuclear know-how. The agreement does not seriously address the parallel path by which Iran can acquire such a capability: The clandestine procurement of components from abroad.

This represents a serious oversight, because Iran maintains active proliferation relationships with a range of suppliers, including the regime of Kim Jong-un in North Korea and private commercial entities in the People's Republic of China. These sources have been essential to Iran's ballistic missile and nuclear advances to date, and can be expected to continue to provide technology and components that enable the Iranian regime to make progress on its nuclear effort in spite of heightened scrutiny over its domestic activities. Moreover, Iran's advances have nudged other countries in the Middle East—most conspicuously Saudi Arabia—to accelerate their own nuclear plans in response. As a result, there is significant potential for a destabilizing "proliferation cascade" in the region in coming years, and of the emergence of multiple nuclear aspirants along Iran's periphery.

Most significantly, however, the Nuclear Deal provides Iran with an economic windfall of unprecedented magnitude. As part of the terms of the JCPOA, the United States and its partners in the P5+1 agreed to release to Iran some $100 billion in previously escrowed oil revenue. As of this writing, Iran has full, unfettered access to these funds, without limitations on their use.

The scope of this economic stimulus is enormous. It amounts to roughly a quarter of Iran's annual GDP, which totaled $415 billion in 2014.[3] That sum rivals the entirety of the European Recovery Program (colloquially known as the Marshall Plan) launched by the Truman administration in 1948 in the aftermath of World War II—an initiative that disbursed $13 billion ($120 billion in today's dollars) to 17 countries in Europe over the span of 4 years. The proportional impact of such relief for Iran is analogous to America's $16.7 trillion economy receiving an infusion of roughly $4.2 trillion—approximately 5 times the stimulus that stabilized the U.S. financial sector following the 2008 global economic crisis.

Moreover, these funds represent only one part of a considerably larger economic picture. While Iran's initial economic windfall will be at least somewhat dampened by the declining global price of oil, the Iranian regime is adapting in response, including by revising its budget downward, focusing on non-oil exports, and significantly expanding domestic taxation.[4] Additionally, the economic stimulus enshrined in the JCPOA will invariably be augmented by the benefits of expanded post-sanctions trade between Iran and countries in Europe and Asia, many of which are now eagerly seeking economic reengagement with the Islamic Republic. This normalization, in turn, is being facilitated by Iran's reintegration into the global financial system via institutions from which it was previously proscribed, such as the Society for Worldwide Interbank Financial Telecommunications (SWIFT).[5]

As a result of these changes, the World Bank now estimates that Iranian GDP will grow by nearly 6 percent this year.[6] Simply put, the JCPOA has laid the groundwork for a sustained economic revival on the part of the Islamic Republic.

ANTICIPATING IRANIAN BEHAVIOR

How is Iran likely to use this economic windfall? The White House has argued that there is little reason for concern, because Iran can be expected to use the funds in question overwhelmingly for domestic reconstruction and economic stabilization,[7]

---

[2] White House, Office of the Press Secretary, "Statement by the President on the Adoption of the Joint Comprehensive Plan of Action," October 18, 2015, *https://www.whitehouse.gov/the-press-office2015/10/18/statement-president-adoption-joint-comprehensive-plan-action.*

[3] "Iran GDP," Trading Economics, n.d., *http://www.tradingeconomics.com/iran/gdp.*

[4] "Iran's 2016 Budget Based on $35–40 Oil a Barrel," AzerNews, December 28, 2015, *http://www.azernews.az/region/91180.html;* "Next FY Budget Focuses on Foreign Capital, Non-Oil Exports," Mehr (Tehran), January 17, 2016, *http://en.mehrnews.com/news/113637/Next-FY-budget-focuses-on-foreign-capital-non-oil-exports.*

[5] "SWIFT to Restart Services to Iran by Jan. 31," *Tehran Times,* January 26, 2016, *http://www.tehrantimes.com/index_View.asp?code=252493.*

[6] "World Bank Forecasts 5.8% GDP Growth for Iran in 2016," *Tehran Times,* February 6, 2016, *http://www.tehrantimes.com/index_View.asp?code=252783.*

[7] Nadia Bilbassy-Charters, "Ben Rhodes: Iran's New Money Post Deal will Go to Uplift 'Terrible Economy,'" *AlArabiya* (Riyadh), July 16, 2015, *http://english.alarabiya.net/en/News/*

and because the total sum available to Iran is considerably less than $100 billion as a result of the Islamic Republic's outstanding debts.[8]

This reasoning is deeply flawed. The U.S. Government's estimate presupposes that the Iranian government will pay back all of its debts before accessing any of the previously-escrowed funds—an unrealistic prospect, particularly in light of the desire of creditor nations (such as China) to engage more deeply in trade with Iran now that sanctions have been lifted. Likewise, the Islamic Republic has a long and well-established history of preferring guns to butter. While some of the funds in question will undoubtedly be allocated for domestic projects, it is reasonable to expect that a portion—and perhaps a significant one—will be used by the regime on key strategic initiatives. These include:

Military modernization

The Islamic Republic is now poised for a period of sustained military expansion. On June 30, 2015, 2 weeks before the formal conclusion of the JCPOA, Iranian Supreme Leader Ali Khamenei formally unveiled his Government's Sixth Development Plan, which outlines an intention to expand the National defense budget by nearly $5 billion, to 5 percent of total GDP.[9] These plans are predicated upon Iran's ability to access additional resources as a result of the JCPOA and post-sanctions trade.

The Islamic Republic, moreover, is already beginning to move in this direction. In recent months, the Iranian regime has initiated new procurement talks for significant quantities of arms and materiel (including new aircraft, air defenses and battlefield components) with both Russia and China. Over time, such acquisitions will lead to a significant strengthening of Iran's ability to project power into its immediate periphery, as well as its capacity to threaten and/or challenge its strategic rivals in the region, as well as American interests there.

Rogue state sponsorship

Although it has received comparatively little attention to date, one of the most significant consequences of the economic windfall inherent in the JCPOA will be its "trickle down" effect on the Islamic Republic's strategic partners. To date, Iran's relations with a host of revanchist and radical regimes—including Venezuela, Bolivia, Ecuador, North Korea, and Sudan, among others—have been constrained, at least in part, by a lack of resources. While Tehran maintains significant political, economic, and military ties with all of those nations, bilateral contacts have been limited by Iran's own economic isolation, as well as by the financial weakness of these rogue state partners themselves.

This, however, may soon change. Given the scope of the sanctions relief contained in the JCPOA, Iran will shortly have the ability to strengthen those alliances significantly. Put simply, Iran has long served as a partner for an array of rogue states and repressive regimes globally. Today, however, Iran for the first time has the potential to serve as their patron—a position that will have pronounced negative effects on global security.

Terrorism financing

Back in 1984, the Reagan administration formally designated Iran as a state sponsor of terrorism for its involvement in, and orchestration of, the October 1983 attack on the U.S. Marine Barracks in Beirut, Lebanon. Today, the Islamic Republic still ranks as the world's foremost sponsor of international terrorism. As recently as this past summer, the Congressional Research Service estimated that the Islamic Republic spent between $3.5 billion to $16 billion annually on support for terrorism and insurgency world-wide.[10] That range encompasses:
- Extensive aid to the regime of Syrian dictator Bashar al-Assad (estimated at some $6 billion annually);
- Material and economic assistance to the Shi'a Houthi rebels in Yemen;
- Support for various Shi'a militias in Iraq;

---

middle-east/2015/07/16/Ben-Rhodes-Iran-s-extra-revenue-after-nuke-deal-will-help-uplift-terrible-economy-.html.

[8] See, for example, "Lew: Iran Not Getting the Full $100 Billion of Frozen Assets," *The Fiscal Times*, July 26, 2015, http://www.thefiscaltimes.com/2015/07/26/Lew-Iran-Not-Getting-Full-100-Billion-Frozen-Assets.

[9] Abbas Qaidaari, "More Planes, Missiles and Warships for Iran," *Al-Monitor*, July 14, 2015, http://www.usnews.com/newsarticles/2015/07/14/more-planes-missiles-and-warships-iran-increases-its-military-budget-by-a-third.

[10] Carla Humud, Christopher Blanchard, Jeremy Sharp, and Jim Zanotti, "Iranian Assistance to Groups in Yemen, Iraq, Syria, and the Palestinian Territories," Congressional Research Service Memorandum, July 31, 2015, http://www.kirk.senate.gov/images/PDF/Iran%20Financial%20Support%20to%20Terrorists%20and%20Militants.pdf.

- The entire operating budget of the Palestinian Islamic Jihad terrorist organization;
- Renewed aid (previously estimated at between $20–25 million monthly) to the Hamas terrorist group; and
- Between $100 and $200 million annually in financial support for Lebanon's Hezbollah militia.

These figures now have the potential to become much, much larger. White House officials have admitted that at least some of Iran's JCPOA-related economic windfall is likely to go to terrorist groups and extremist causes.[11] That, however, represents something of an understatement; given the size of the immediate sanctions relief at its disposal, should Iran allocate a mere 10 percent of its recently-unfrozen funds to such activities, it could double or even triple its current spending on terror sponsorship.

Regional expansionism

The past several years have seen the Islamic Republic embark upon an ambitious, multi-pronged effort to reshape the region in its own image. This effort has included, inter alia, attempts to undermine the monarchy in Bahrain; extensive backing for Yemen's Houthi insurgency; both financial and direct military assistance to the Assad regime in Syria, and; broad geopolitical support for Iraq's Shi'a militias. It has been animated by the Iranian leadership's conviction that, in the words of Iranian Supreme Leader Ali Khamenei himself, the international system is "in the process of change" and a "new order is being formed."[12] The message is unmistakable; Iran's leaders believe that declining Western influence provides their country with the opportunity to expand its reach and power in the Middle East.

The Iranian regime now has far greater ability to do so. Empowered by the resources inherent in the JCPOA, as well as the permissive political environment that has been created as a result, recent months have seen the Iranian regime adopt an increasingly expansionist foreign policy line. The consequences can be felt in deepening Iranian-Saudi tensions, multiple ballistic missile tests in violation of U.N. Security Council resolutions, and a more aggressive military posture in the Persian Gulf. These actions reflect the belief among Iranian policymakers, like Alaeddin Boroujerdi, chairman of the Iranian parliament's national security and foreign policy committee, that the security of the Persian Gulf is now "in Iran's hands."[13]

As the narrative above lays out, the expanded resources conferred by the JCPOA have the potential to dramatically increase the strategic capabilities of the Iranian regime—and, consequently, the threat it poses to international security. In the context of the United States homeland, these dangers are likely to be most pronounced in 2 distinct arenas.

AN EXPANDING FOOTPRINT IN LATIN AMERICA

The past decade has seen a systematic expansion of the Islamic Republic's strategic presence in the Americas. Using the sympathetic regime of Hugo Chavez in Venezuela as a gateway, Iran has dramatically broadened its diplomatic ties to the region, focusing in particular on the countries of the leftist political bloc known as the Bolivarian Alliance of the Americas (ALBA). Since 2005, Iran has nearly doubled the number of its embassies in the region, from 6 to 11.[14] Its economic ties to the region have similarly ballooned, in particular its trade with the nations of Brazil, Bolivia, and Ecuador.

This formal outreach has been mirrored by the establishment of a formidable asymmetric presence. Iran's informal activities in the region date back to the early 1980s, when it facilitated a foothold for its chief terrorist proxy, Hezbollah, in the so-called Tri-Border Region where Brazil, Argentina, and Paraguay intersect. That presence, in turn, made possible the massive July 1994 bombing of the Argentine—Israel Mutual Association (AMIA) in Buenos Aires—an attack that Argentine state

---

[11] See, for example, Matthew Lee, "Kerry: Some Iran Sanctions Relief Likely to Go to Terrorists," Associated Press, January 21, 2016, *http://bigstory.ap.org/article/9ab669cada3b47cfaa3e6793a3ca6faa/kerry-rejects-iranian-criticism-us-sanctions.*

[12] Arash Karami, "Ayatollah Khamenei Urges Iran to Prepare for 'New World Order,'" *Al-Monitor,* September 5, 2014, *http://www.al-monitor.com/pulse/originals/2014/09/khamenei-new-world-order.html#.*

[13] "Persian Gulf Security in Iran's Hands: Senior MP," Tasnim (Tehran), January 14, 2016, *http://www.tasnimnews.com/en/news/2016/01/14/971145/persian-gulf-security-in-iran-s-hands-senior-mp.*

[14] Iran today boasts an official diplomatic presence in Argentina, Bolivia, Brazil, Chile, Colombia, Cuba, Ecuador, Mexico, Nicaragua, Uruguay and Venezuela.

prosecutors subsequently concluded had been "ordered by the highest authorities of the Islamic Republic of Iran in conjunction with Hezbollah."[15]

Three decades on, Iran's asymmetric presence in the region is more extensive—and arguably far more lethal. As the late Argentine prosecutor Alberto Nisman detailed in his May 2013 indictment, over the past 3 decades Iran has successfully created a network of intelligence bases and covert centers in no fewer than 8 Latin American countries: Brazil, Paraguay, Uruguay, Chile, Colombia, Guyana, Trinidad and Tobago, and Suriname.[16] This infrastructure has enabled Iran to initiate or support at least 3 separate plots against the U.S. homeland over the past decade.

- A 2007 plot involving Guyanese national Abdul Kadir to blow up fuel tanks underneath New York's John F. Kennedy Airport. According to Nisman, Kadir was a disciple and agent of Iranian cleric Mohsen Rabbani, the alleged mastermind of the 1994 AMIA bombing, and had previously "carried out the Iranian infiltration in Guyana" at Rabbani's direction.[17] Had it succeeded, the attempt would have caused "extensive damage to the airport and to the New York economy, as well as the loss of numerous lives," the FBI assessed.[18]
- An October 2011 attempt by Iran's Revolutionary Guard Corps (IRGC) to assassinate Saudi Arabia's ambassador to the United States at a D.C. restaurant, using members of Mexico's Los Zetas drug cartel to carry out the killing. In a press conference divulging details of the failed scheme, Attorney General Eric Holder noted that it was "directed and approved by elements of the Iranian government and, specifically, senior members of the Quds Force," the IRGC's elite paramilitary unit.[19]
- A plan by Venezuelan and Iranian diplomats to use Mexican hackers to penetrate U.S. defense, intelligence and nuclear facilities and launch wide-spread cyber attacks throughout the United States. The effort was detailed in a December 2011 investigative documentary by the Spanish-language TV network *Univision*, which featured audio recordings of the plotters, including a high-ranking Iranian diplomat.[20] In the wake of the documentary's airing, Venezuela's consul general to Miami was declared persona non grata and expelled from the country.[21]

Hezbollah's presence in the Americas has likewise continued to grow apace. Over the past several years, a string of incidents—among them the November 2014 apprehension of a Hezbollah operative in Lima, Peru; regional intelligence reports about Hezbollah activity in Mexico, Nicaragua, Chile, Colombia, Bolivia, and Ecuador; and revelations about official Venezuelan facilitation of the movement of Hezbollah operatives throughout the region via the provision of state-issued passports[22]—all point to a significant operational presence on the part of the terrorist group south of the U.S. border.

The risks to American security posed by this expanding footprint are both clear and present. Iran has already demonstrated both the capability and the intent to target the U.S. homeland, directly and via its proxies, through the Latin American theater. The capability for Iran to do so can be expected to grow in the near future. Given the priority attention that has been paid to Latin America by Iran in recent years, it is reasonable to expect that the Iranian regime will use its expanded resources to broaden and further solidify its footprint in the Western Hemisphere. If

[15] Marcelo Martinez Burgos and Alberto Nisman, "AMIA Case," Investigations Unit of the Office of the Attorney General, 2006, *http://www.peaceandtolerance.org/docs/nismanindict.pdf*.

[16] Guido Nejamkis, "Iran Set Up Terrorist Networks in Latin America: Argentine Prosecutor," Reuters, May 29, 2013, *http://www.reuters.com/article/2013/05/29/us-argentina-iran-idUSBRE94S1F420130529*.

[17] Ibid.

[18] Federal Bureau of Investigation, New York Field Office, "Abdul Kadir Sentenced to Life in Prison for Conspiring to Commit Terrorist Attack at JFK Airport," December 15, 2010, *http://www.fbi.gov/newyork/press-releases/2010/nyfo121510a.htm*.

[19] Charles Savage and Scott Shane, "Iranians Accused of a Plot to Kill Saudis' U.S. Envoy," *New York Times*, October 11, 2011, *http://www.nytimes.com/2011/10/12/us/us-accuses-iranians-of-plotting-to-kill-saudi-envoy.html?pagewanted=all*.

[20] "La Amenaza Irani," *Univision*, December 9, 2011, *http://noticias.univision.com/article/786870/2011-12-09/documentales/la-amenaza-irani/la-amenaza-irani*.

[21] "U.S. Expels Venezuelan Diplomat in Miami," CNN, January 9, 2014, *http://www.cnn.com/2012/01/08/us/venezuela-consul/*.

[22] Barak Ravid, "Hezbollah Member Held in Peru for Planning Terror Attack," *Ha'aretz* (Tel Aviv), October 30, 2014, *http://www.haaretz.com/world-news/.premium-1.623743*: "Latin America Takes Action to Control Hezbollah's Activities," *Asharq Al-Awsat* (London), January 25, 2016, *http://english.aawsat.com/2016/01/article55346877/latin-america-takes-action-to-control-hezbollahs-activities*: "Venezuela Exposes the Involvement of Hezbollah and Iran in the Americas," *Janoubia*, January 27, 2016, *http://janoubia.com/2016/01/27/[sic]*.

history is any judge, it will do so in a way that will be deeply inimical to American interests.

Cyber space is fast emerging as a new domain of conflict between Iran and the West. Beginning in the fall of 2010, Iran's nuclear program was targeted by the Stuxnet computer worm, waking Iranian officials up to the fact that the West was attempting to compromise their nuclear effort. Subsequent attacks on Iranian nuclear facilities and infrastructure convinced Iran's leadership that cyber war had the potential to be—in the words of one top regime official—"more dangerous than a physical war."[23]

Iran mobilized in response. In July 2011, the regime formally launched an ambitious $1 billion governmental program to boost national cyber capabilities via the acquisition of new technologies, new investments in cyber defense, and the creation of a new cadre of cyber experts.[24] In tandem, it formed new, dedicated domestic agencies tasked with administering cyber space, as well as creating a dedicated Cyber Defense Command within the Iranian military and an analogous Cyberspace Council in the basij, the country's repressive domestic militia.[25] Simultaneously, the Iranian government mobilized a "cyber army" of activists—nominally independent patriotic hackers (also known as "hacktivists") who have carried out attacks on sites and entities out of favor with the Iranian regime, including social networking platform Twitter, the Chinese search engine Baidu, and the websites of Iranian reformist elements.[26] The Intelligence Unit of Iran's clerical army, the Iranian Revolutionary Guard Corps (IRGC) allegedly oversees the activities of this "cyber army."[27]

Iran likewise has harnessed this growing capability against the West. The past several years have seen a range of aggressive—and increasingly capable—Iranian attacks on Western and allied interests via cyber space.

- In the summer of 2012, Saudi Arabia's state oil giant, ARAMCO, was hit by an Iranian-developed virus called "Shamoon" that compromised three-quarters of the company's computers.[28]
- Between September 2012 and January 2013, multiple U.S. financial institutions (including Bank of America, JPMorgan Chase, and Citigroup) experienced a series of distributed denial-of-service (DDoS) attacks that disrupted their on-line presence and functionality. Due to the sophistication of the attacks, U.S. officials linked them definitively to the Iranian government.[29]
- In October 2013, the U.S. Navy's unclassified computer network was penetrated by hackers affiliated with the Iranian government, potentially compromising email and secure communications hosted on it.[30]
- In February 2014, the Nevada-based Sands Corporation experienced a computer attack that temporarily crippled its systems, an intrusion that has since been conclusively linked to Iran by the U.S. intelligence community.[31]
- In May 2014, cyber intelligence firm iSight Partners uncovered a complex Iranian "phishing" scheme dubbed "Newscaster," which was designed to com-

---

[23] "Iran Sees Cyber Attacks as Greater Threat than Actual War," Reuters, September 25, 2012, *http://www.reuters.com/article/2012/09/25/net-us-iran-military-idUSBRE88Q0MY-20120925.*

[24] Yaakov Katz, "Iran Embarks On $1b. Cyber-Warfare Program," *Jerusalem Post,* December 18, 2011, *http://www.jpost.com/Defense/Article.aspx?id=249864.*

[25] See, for example, Kevin Lim, "Iran's Cyber Posture," *OpenBriefing,* November 18, 2013, *http://www.openbriefing.org/regionaldesks/middleeast/irans-cyber-posture/.*

[26] Farvartish Rezvaniyeh, "Pulling the Strings of the Net: Iran's Cyber Army," PBS Frontline, February 26, 2010, *http://www.pbs.org/wgbh/pages/frontline/tehranbureau/2010/02/pulling-the-strings-of-the-net-irans-cyber-army.html*; Alex Lukich, "The Iranian Cyber Army," Center for Strategic & International Studies, July 12, 2011, *http://csis.org/blog/iranian-cyber-army.*

[27] University of Pennsylvania, Annenberg School of Communications, Iran Media Program, "Internet Censorship in Iran," n.d., *http://iranmediaresearch.org/sites/default/files/research/pdf/1363180689/1385/intern_et_censorship_in_iran.pdf.*

[28] Nicole Perlroth, "In Cyberattack on Saudi Firm, U.S. Sees Iran Firing Back," *New York Times,* October 23, 2012, *http://www.nytimes.com/2012/10/24/business/global/cyberattack-on-saudi-oil-firm-disquiets-us.html?pagewanted=all.*

[29] Nicole Perlroth and Quentin Hardy, "Bank Hacking Was the Work of Iranians, Officials Say," *New York Times,* January 8, 2013, *http://www.nytimes.com/2013/01/09/technology/online-banking-attacks-were-work-of-iran-us-officials-say.html?pagewanted=1&_r=0.*

[30] Julian E. Barnes and Siobhan Gorman, "U.S. Says Iran Hacked Navy Computers," *Wall Street Journal,* September 27, 2013, *http://www.wsj.com/articles/SB10001424052702304526204579101602356751772.*

[31] Tony Capaccio, David Lerman, and Chris Strohm, "Iran Behind Cyber-Attack on Adelson's Sands Corp., Clapper Says," Bloomberg, February 26, 2015, *http://www.bloomberg.com/news/articles/2015-02-26/iran-behind-cyber-attack-on-adelson-s-sands-corp-clapper-says.*

promise prominent political individuals of interest to the Islamic Republic
through the use of social media.[32]
- In the spring of 2014, Iranian hacking group Ajax Security Team was found to
have targeted U.S. defense firms with malicious software in order to gain access
to their computers.[33]
- Iranian hackers are known to have extensively mapped U.S. infrastructure
points, such as the power grid, trains, airlines and refineries, in what cyber experts fear could be a hostile contingency scenario in the event of a conflict with
America.[34]
- Most recently, Iranian hackers carried out an extensive campaign of intelligence
gathering aimed at the U.S. State Department in November 2015.[35] The effort
included targeting diplomats with responsibility for Iran and the Middle East
via both email and social media as part of what U.S. officials say is an increasingly aggressive attempt to glean information about American policies toward
the Islamic Republic.

The scope of Iran's offensive cyber activities was outlined in detail in a December
2014 report by San Diego-based cybersecurity firm Cylance, which stated that:
"Since at least 2012, Iranian actors have directly attacked, established persistence
in, and extracted highly sensitive materials from the networks of government agencies and major critical infrastructure companies in the following countries: Canada,
China, England, France, Germany, India, Israel, Kuwait, Mexico, Pakistan, Qatar,
Saudi Arabia, South Korea, Turkey, United Arab Emirates, and the United
States."[36] Targets of Iranian cyber attack identified by Cylance include oil and gas
firms in Kuwait, Turkey, Qatar and France, aviation hubs in South Korea and Pakistan, energy and utilities companies in Canada and the United States, and government agencies in the United States, UAE, and Qatar.

Moreover, the study suggests, this may represent merely the tip of the iceberg.
"As Iran's cyber warfare capabilities continue to morph . . . the probability of an
attack that could impact the physical world at a national or global level is rapidly
increasing," it concludes.[37]

Today, that warning is more salient than ever. Between 2014 and 2015, Iran—
eager to reap the benefits of nuclear detente with the West—noticeably scaled back
its on-line targeting of the West. But in the wake of this summer's Nuclear Deal,
the Islamic Republic is ramping up its offensive cyber activities anew, for both political and strategic reasons. Domestically, Iran's hard-liners are at pains to assert
their primacy in national affairs following the nuclear agreement—including over
the regime's strategic programs, of which cyber space is one. Abroad, Iranian leaders have increasingly come to see cyber space as an indispensable domain for strategic influence, one that has risen in importance now that their country's nuclear
program is at least temporarily constrained.

Given this emphasis, as well as the economic benefits of the JCPOA—which will
increase the resources available to the regime to invest in its strategic capabilities—
the Islamic Republic is poised to become an increasingly mature and formidable
cyber power. In the process, it will invariably emerge as a serious cyber challenge
for the United States.

LOOKING AHEAD

Since the start of nuclear diplomacy in November of 2013, the Obama administration has effectively downplayed the risks emanating from Iran. In its eagerness to
conclude some sort of agreement with Iran over its nuclear program, the White
House has systematically turned a blind eye to the Islamic Republic's fomentation
of international terrorism, its support for rogue foreign regimes, and its strategic activities.

---

[32] Mike Lennon, "Iranian Hackers Targeted US Officials in Elaborate Social Media Attack Operation," Security Week, May 29, 2014, *http://www.securityweek.com/iranian-hackers-targeted-
us-officials-elaborate-social-media-attack-operation.*
[33] Dune Lawrence, "Iranian Hackers, Getting More Sophisticated, Target U.S. Defense Companies," Bloomberg, May 14, 2014, *http://www.bloomberg.com/bw/articles/2014-05-14/iranian-
hackers-getting-more-sophisticated-target-u-dot-s-dot-defense-companies.*
[34] Brian Ross, "What Will Happen to the US if Israel Attacks Iran?" ABC News, March 5,
2012, *http://abcnews.go.com/Blotter/israel-attacks-iran-gas-prices-cyberwar-terror-threat/
story?id=15848522#.T4g5tqvY9Ll.*
[35] David E. Sanger and Nicole Perlroth, "Iranian Hackers Attack State Dept. via Social Media
Accounts," *New York Times,* November 24, 2015, *http://www.nytimes.com/2015/11/25/world/
middleeast/iran-hackers-cyberespionage-state-department-social-media.html.*
[36] Cylance, Operation Cleaver, December 2, 2014, *http://www.cylance.com/assets/Cleaver/
Cylance_Operation_Cleaver_Report.pdf.*
[37] Ibid.

Now that implementation of the JCPOA has begun, Iran's capabilities in all of these areas have the potential to expand dramatically—and to do so to the detriment of American security. Tracking this growing destructive potential must become a top priority of the U.S. Government. So, too, must the formulation of a strategy to identify, manage, and limit Iranian rogue behavior in the years ahead.

Mr. KING. Our next witness is Mr. Bilal Saab. He is the resident senior fellow for Middle East Security with the Brent Scowcroft Center on International Security. He also serves on the board of several research organizations, excuse me, in the United States and the Middle East.

He has received awards from the Atlantic Council and from the Center for Strategic and International Studies. He has previously worked at the Institute for Near East and Gulf Military Analysis, the Sabin Center for Middle East Policy at Brookings, and the Center for the Study of Terrorism and Political Violence at the University of St. Andrews in the United Kingdom.

He has a B.A. from the American University of Beirut, a master's in International Security Studies from the University of St. Andrews, and a M.A. in International Security Policy from the University of Maryland.

With that, I am pleased to welcome you and look forward to your testimony. Congratulations, again, on the newborn. Everybody healthy and everything fine? Great. Good. Okay.

STATEMENT OF BILAL Y. SAAB, SENIOR FELLOW FOR MIDDLE EAST SECURITY, BRENT SCOWCROFT CENTER ON INTERNATIONAL SECURITY, ATLANTIC COUNCIL

Mr. SAAB. Thank you, Mr. Chairman and Mr. Higgins. I am grateful for the opportunity to testify today on this very important subject. Once again, thank you for the congratulations.

If you asked me what is the biggest accomplishment of Iranian foreign policy since the 1979 revolution, I would say, in my judgment, it would be the contribution to the creation and subsequent development of Hezbollah, the Lebanese Shiite party.

Hezbollah, today, is one of the most powerful subnational actors operating in the world today. It has got global reach. It has got intelligence, counter-intelligence, military capabilities that are probably more significant than many mid-sized European countries. It has got regional political clout that, I would say, tops that of many Middle Eastern governments.

The main question today that many Hezbollah watchers are grappling with is whether the group's local and regional position has been strengthened or weakened, as a result of its over-involvement in the Syrian conflict.

So let me give you my bottom line right up front. The Syrian conflict presents Hezbollah with the biggest challenge it has faced since it was born, but it also creates opportunities. Let's be very honest about that.

Let me address just a couple of scenarios, as far as Hezbollah and how that affects the organization. The worst-case scenario for Hezbollah, as far as Syria is concerned, is, of course, the rebels winning and the fall of the regime. But I would say that even that, although it would make its life extremely difficult, it would not end it.

The best-case scenario, of course, would be a total defeat of the rebels. Also, to be honest, it is not really unthinkable, in today's circumstances. As a result of that, it would help the organization cement its control of Lebanon and further assert itself regionally.

The middle-ground scenario, which is the continuation of the status quo, and neither the regime nor the rebels win, yes, it would make its life, also, difficult. It will be costly for the organization. It prolongs the Syrian spillover into Lebanon. But it has made a lot of adjustments, and it has been quite successful at that, as well.

So why is it, actually, that, regardless of what happens in Syria, the organization will survive? I would say that the two main sources of support of the organization, that matter more than anything else, quite frankly, will remain intact. That is the Shiite support base of the organization, which, you know, they have cultivated for a very long time, since 1982, ever since their founding.

Of course, it is their main patron, Iran. Those two sources of support will endure, no matter what happens in Syria. You can make an argument that the bond between Hezbollah and its constituency has been under pressure, because of its costly adventure in Syria. But I haven't really seen any significant cracks in the bond.

As far as the special relationship it has with Iran, it will also endure. Why? Because the partnership has been extremely beneficial for both sides.

As you know, Mr. Chairman, Iran provides Hezbollah with money, weapons, strategic direction, organizational coherence, you name it. In return, Hezbollah allows Iran to reject Shiite power in the Arab world, and, with its military arsenal, it helps deter Israel from attacking Iran.

I have every reason to believe that these relations between the two allies, Hezbollah and Iran, will continue to develop, following the lifting of sanctions against Tehran, which brings me to Hezbollah's international activities, because, at the end of the day, they are an extension, in my opinion, of the paramilitary and intelligence agencies of Iran. They are not really independent.

So will the threat the group poses to the homeland increase, decrease, remain the same after the lifting of sanctions and, specifically, when Tehran has a few more billions of dollars to spend? I would say that any serious assessment has to look at both the intentions of the organization, but also the capabilities.

You know, having interacted, throughout my career, with many officials and analysts within the intelligence community regarding Hezbollah, I would say that nobody doubts the capabilities of the organization. It is just on the issue of intentions where there might be some debate.

Two reasons why Hezbollah has never really acted or attacked on U.S. territory: First, Hezbollah does not really strategize or act alone, when it comes to global operations. Tehran is in charge, here, for sure.

The second reason, Hezbollah has no interest, itself, because it is well—much aware of its own limitations and the consequences, the steep consequences, for taking on the most powerful nation on earth.

Now, could this change in the foreseeable future? I think a lot of it would depend on the evolution of relations between Iran and the United States. Should those—you know, should the relations take a dramatic turn for the worse, over a number of scenarios, it is likely that Iran might fight back, using asymmetric tools and particularly terrorism.

One of those tools may well be Hezbollah, of course. But, I would say, even under that scenario, Hezbollah would think twice, really, before it would decide to pick this fight, from which, really, it probably would not survive.

The U.S. Government has designated Hezbollah as a terrorist organization, but, in my mind, I think that terrorism is only one of the challenges that the organization poses. As a matter of fact, it is not the most imminent, it is not the most significant, in my opinion. The counterterrorism lens is a little bit too narrow.

The party, at the end of the day, is a product of Lebanon's internal weakness, Iran's intervention in Lebanese politics, previously Syria, and, of course, the on-going conflict with Israel. So the United States really has no desire or capacity to solve all these complex problems.

They have been—you know, they have been present for a very long time. I wrote, almost 6 years ago, and I think it is still pertinent today, that the most affordable option the United States can pursue, as far as Hezbollah, is containment, really.

You know, Washington should continue to provide assistance to the Lebanese armed forces, which it is doing, and try to bolster the country's internal strength, which would, ultimately, diminish the group's rationale for keeping its arms.

In closing, Mr. Chairman, let me emphasize that Hezbollah is dealing with really significant pressures, as a result of its costly intervention in Syria. The adjustments it has been forced to make have not been easy at all.

But the succession that these pressures represent, that the pressures will really lead to its death, in my opinion, represents nothing but wishful thinking. Equally important, it doesn't seem like its adversaries, foreign and domestic, are really in a position to take advantage of its present travails.

So this transformation that it is going through, from a domestic hegemon of Lebanon into a regional powerhouse, quite frankly, is now more achievable, because of what is happening in Syria.

Thank you, very much.

[The prepared statement of Mr. Saab follows:]

PREPARED STATEMENT OF BILAL Y. SAAB

FEBRUARY 11, 2016

Chairman King, Subcommittee Ranking Member Higgins, full Committee Ranking Member Thompson, distinguished Members of the subcommittee, I am grateful for the opportunity to testify today on this very important subject.[1]

If one were to identify the biggest accomplishment of Iranian foreign policy since the 1979 Islamic revolution, it would be, in my judgment, the direct contribution to the creation and subsequent development of Hezbollah, the Lebanese Shi'ite party. I believe that Hezbollah is one of the most powerful sub-national militant actors operating in the world today. It has global reach; intelligence, counterintelligence, and

---

[1] This testimony draws on my research work in Lebanon, my scholarship on Hezbollah, and on a recently co-authored paper with Dr. Daniel Byman, "Hezbollah in a Time of Transition" (Washington, DC: Atlantic Council and Brookings, November 2014) *http://www.atlanticcouncil.org/images/publications/Hezbollah_in_a_Time_of_Transition.pdf.*

military capabilities that are more significant than many mid-sized European countries; and regional political clout that tops that of many Middle Eastern governments.

The main question that is on the minds of Hezbollah observers is whether the group's domestic and regional position has been strengthened or weakened as a result of its overt involvement in the Syrian conflict. That is what I will focus on in my testimony today. My bottom line is that while the war in Syria presents Hezbollah with the biggest challenge it has faced since it was born, it also creates opportunities. The worst-case scenario of Damascus falling into the hands of the rebels—a scenario that currently looks improbable—will make Hezbollah's life extremely difficult, but it will not end it. At the other extreme, should the rebels suffer a total defeat, Hezbollah would further assert itself regionally and cement its control of Lebanon. The continuation of the status quo, where neither the Syrian opposition nor the regime wins and the civil war goes on, will not lead to Hezbollah's demise either. An indefinite stalemate is costly for Hezbollah because it does not solve the problem of Syrian spillover, it prolongs political tensions in Beirut, and it keeps Lebanon and Hezbollah's Shi'ite supporters at risk of attack by Sunni extremists—but it also does not force Hezbollah and Iran to make drastic decisions and tough compromises.

So regardless of what happens in Syria, Hezbollah will most probably survive if it continues to effectively nurture and manage two critical relationships: Its Shi'ite support base and its main patron, Iran. These 2 sources of support matter more to the well-being of the organization than anything else. Currently, neither relationship looks volatile. While the bond between Hezbollah and its constituency is under pressure due to the group's costly intervention in Syria, cracks have yet to emerge. Growing instability and Sunni extremist violence in the region may have even strengthened ties between Hezbollah and its Shi'ite supporters. As for the group's deep and organic link to Iran, it will most likely endure and become stronger following the lifting of international sanctions against Tehran and the inflow of cash to the Islamic Revolutionary Guard Corps (IRGC), Hezbollah's primary ally within the Iranian government.

Hezbollah's future has important implications for Lebanon, the region's stability, and U.S. interests and those of its partners in the Middle East. The Syrian conflict has forced Hezbollah to transition into something it does not necessarily desire or is able to sustain. A movement that long claimed to transcend sectarianism has become a bogeyman to many of the region's Sunni Muslims. At the same time, Hezbollah's deep involvement in the fighting in Syria has damaged its reputation in Lebanon and made it a target of Sunni extremist violence. The conflict with Israel, while still a focus of rhetoric, has somewhat faded to the background. However, the suggestion that the significant pressures Hezbollah is dealing with will ultimately lead to its death represents nothing but wishful thinking. The party is more resilient than its adversaries would like to admit. That the tide of the war in Syria seems to be turning in its favor also provides comfort for the organization.

My testimony contains 4 parts. I begin by describing various storms that Hezbollah effectively weathered in the past and explain how it did so. I then devote two sections to analyze how events in the region over the past 5 years and particularly the conflict in Syria present challenges as well as opportunities to the group. I conclude by discussing the policy implications and recommendations for the United States.

PAST STORMS

Hezbollah's death has been proclaimed numerous times since its inception in the early 1980s, but the Shi'ite party has survived numerous challenges: 3 high-intensity military conflicts with Israel in 1993, 1996, and 2006; Israel's assassination of several of its core leaders, including Sheikh Ragheb Harb in 1984, Abbas Al-Musawi in 1992, and Imad Mughniyeh in 2008; the Syrian departure from Lebanon in 2005; a non-stop war of intelligence and counterintelligence against Israel; various political crises in Beirut; an international tribunal investigating the February 2005 murder of former Lebanese Prime Minister Rafik Hariri that formally accused four Hezbollah members; and Arab uprisings that profoundly challenged its philosophy of "champion of the downtrodden, underprivileged, and disenfranchised."

How Hezbollah has survived all these crises can be attributed to a number of internal and external factors, including leadership, organizational coherence and discipline, political violence and tactics, superior training, and, of course, Syrian assistance. But all this would count for little without the constant support Hezbollah receives from its Shi'ite constituency and from Iran. Unlike many other non-state actors in the region, Hezbollah has a domestic base of support about which it cares deeply, and this concern is reciprocated. The organization has made it a top priority to cultivate good relations with the Lebanese Shi'a, knowing full well that such ties would serve as its first and last lines of defense. Iran not only provides religious guidance and strategic direction to Hezbollah, but also helps the party solidify its bond with its constituency through money and weapons.

CHALLENGES

By intervening in Syria to come to Syrian President Bashar Assad's aid, Hassan Nasrallah, Hezbollah's Secretary General, has put his party on a collision course with Sunnis—moderates and extremists alike—in Syria and Lebanon, and elsewhere in the region. This course of action is very risky for Hezbollah and its constituency because regional demographics have always worked against the Shi'ites. Even the staunchest Lebanese Shi'ite supporters of Hezbollah would prefer peace with their fellow Sunni Lebanese—and the region—to conflict. It is not just that Sunni radicals, despite Hezbollah's military advances in Syria, have been able to penetrate deep into the Shi'ite party's sphere of influence and wreak havoc. More importantly, the same extremists who Nasrallah was hoping to fight outside Lebanon could turn Lebanon into another Iraq, a country defined by Sunni-Shi'ite sectarian violence. In this scenario, whose chances are unclear, Hezbollah stands to lose the most, because another Lebanese civil war would be a major distraction from the military struggle against Israel.[2]

At home, Hezbollah may have contained the effects of the Special Tribunal for Lebanon (STL), but the international institution has already caused considerable damage to the party's reputation by instilling serious doubts, even among Hezbollah's friends, about the party's role in killing Rafik Hariri, the former Lebanese prime minister and leader of the Sunni community in the country, in addition to several other anti-Syrian Lebanese politicians, journalists, and security personnel.[3]

More broadly, the Arab uprisings have arguably made Hezbollah less relevant in Arab political discourse. While the concept of resistance against Israel will always generate strong emotions and resonate deeply in the Arab world, such a struggle, an increasing number of Arabs now believe, cannot be at the expense of freedom and political-economic rights. Hezbollah and Iran clearly think otherwise; for them, nothing takes precedence over the military struggle because no other form of resistance works. The group's intervention in Syria has shattered its image in the Arab street. Although such a street has always been polarized, the average Arab person, not too long ago, used to adore the party for standing up to Israel and the United States. Not anymore. Hezbollah's flags are being burned in Syria and elsewhere.[4]

Hezbollah's fight in Syria also has made it more vulnerable toward Israel. Another war with Israel may pump life into Hezbollah's hard-core cadres and add fire to its resistance approach, but in reality such an extremely risky adventure could entail massive costs from which the group may not recover easily this time around. Iran could immediately send money for reconstruction purposes like it did after the end of the 2006 war, but that is not inevitable. And the Syrian regime, busy fighting for its life, may not be operationally capable of providing necessary military and logistical support during any such war.

For Hezbollah, the military challenge in Syria is more daunting than in the Lebanese theater. In contrast to southern Lebanon, Hezbollah forces do not have an intimate knowledge of the Syrian terrain. In addition, they must cooperate with irregular and regular Syrian forces and Iraqi militias, rather than just rely on their own fighters. Hezbollah frequently operates at the company and even battalion level in Syria, using far larger formations than it usually has had in Lebanon when it waged guerilla war against Israel. As Islamic State fighters advanced in Iraq, many of the Iraqi Shi'ite militias aiding the Assad regime went home to fight, increasing the burden on Hezbollah. Because of its heavy role in Syria, Hezbollah is more militarily invested in Iran than ever before. In Syria, the IRGC's Quds Force assisted Hezbollah with command and control and training. Entering the war was in part "payback" for past favors—but by doing so, Hezbollah tied itself even more tightly to its Iranian master. Finally, Hezbollah also has a military role in Lebanon. Along

---

[2] Daniel Byman and Bilal Y. Saab, "Hezbollah Hesitates? The Group's Uncertain Transformation," *Foreign Affairs*, January 21, 2015 *https://www.foreignaffairs.com/articles/israel/2015-01-21/hezbollah-hesitates.*

[3] Bilal Y. Saab, "Why Lebanon's Najib Mikati Resigned: Hezbollah Makes Its Move," *Foreign Affairs*, March 25, 2013 *https://www.foreignaffairs.com/articles/lebanon/2013-03-25/why-lebanons-najib-mikati-resigned.*

[4] Bilal Y. Saab, "Ominous New Struggle for Hezbollah," *The National Interest*, October 24, 2011 *http://nationalinterest.org/commentary/ominous-new-struggle-hezbollah-6060.*

the Syria-Lebanon border, its forces are patrolling and even laying mines in order to prevent infiltration by fighters belonging to the Islamic State and Jabhat al-Nusra. Hezbollah coordinates quietly with the Lebanese Armed Forces, which dare not confront the Shi'ite group.

If Assad's regime collapses, Hezbollah would lose a key supporter from a country that historically has played a dominant role in Lebanese politics. Even more important, Syria is Iran's closest ally, and Tehran was calling in its chits by asking Hezbollah and other supporters to close ranks around the Assad regime. Should Syria fall, Hezbollah is likely to lose a transit route and storage facility for weapons from Iran and Syria. In anticipation of any rapid deterioration of security conditions in Syria, Hezbollah has reportedly moved hundreds of missiles from storage sites in Syria to bases in eastern Lebanon. The potential loss of its logistics hub and supply line in Syria would place Hezbollah at a significant disadvantage in the event of another conflict with Israel. In the 2006 conflict with Israel, the group benefited from the strategic transit route through Syria, which allowed Hezbollah to quickly replenish its weapons supplies; therefore, the loss of Syrian support could cause Hezbollah to hold onto its larger, strategic weapons if they cannot be easily acquired and replaced. Unless Hezbollah and Iran can build a similar capability in another location, Hezbollah will likely face challenges resupplying its rockets and missiles in the near term.

But should Assad leave—or even should his jihadist opponents grow stronger—the gravest threat Hezbollah (and Lebanon as a whole) would have to imminently deal with is Sunni extremism. Sunni radicals would not settle for controlling Syria, but would also seek to expand into Lebanon (and possibly Jordan) to fulfill their ideological goals and go after Hezbollah and its Shi'ite supporters. Over the past year, Sunni jihadists have attacked Shi'ite interests in Lebanon on multiple occasions (the bombing of the Iranian embassy on November 19, 2013, was the most spectacular, killing 23 people and injuring dozens more). Hezbollah, with the help of the Lebanese army, has shown resiliency and has currently managed to contain the threat by battling with Sunni militants across the Syrian-Lebanese borders and in various areas in Lebanon's northern region, and forcing many of them to retreat into Syria. But the fight is anything but over. Hezbollah is not oblivious to the risks and costs of its military intervention in Syria. Its leadership has calculated that, so long as the balance of power tilts in favor of Assad's forces and the Syria-Lebanon border is largely secure, the costs of siding with Syria are tolerable. However, if the situation drastically worsens in Syria, the costs of supporting what could be a falling regime will be much higher for Hezbollah. Therefore, it is possible the group will revisit its policy to defend its core interests—protecting its arms supplies, maintaining its military deterrent posture vis-á-vis Israel, and aiding Iran should it come under attack.

Without the continuous support of Iran and Syria, Hezbollah would not have been able to dominate Lebanese politics, build a state within a state, and become a formidable regional force. But the same ties that have transformed Hezbollah and increased its powers over the years have also brought significant costs to the organization in terms of lives, resources, reputation, and political standing both in Lebanon and the region. Hezbollah's military intervention in Syria is a clear example of how the group's strategic links to Damascus and Tehran, which have served it so well over the years, can also be a great burden.

OPPORTUNITIES

The existing tensions within Hezbollah's camp are real, though they should not be exaggerated. Shi'a sentiment in Lebanon is still very much pro-Hezbollah and it would take a long time for Shi'ite dissent and dissatisfaction with the group's entry into Syria to shake its grip on the community. After all, Hezbollah has been nurturing these ties since 1982, providing the Lebanese Shi'a with social goods, a political voice, security, and a sense of empowerment. Nor is there a strong rival movement. Perhaps most important, the slaughter of minorities by the Islamic State and its bloodthirsty anti-Shi'ite rhetoric create a sense that Hezbollah had no choice but to aid Assad—that it was a case of kill or be killed.

With every bomb that goes off in its stronghold—and with every loss of Shi'a life that is not caused by Israel-Hezbollah's control of its support base could wane, but it will not drastically diminish.[5] Hezbollah's relations with the Shi'ite Amal and the

---

[5] Bilal Y. Saab, "Hezbollah Under Fire: Could the Bombing in Beirut Spell the End of the Shia Group?," *Foreign Affairs*, November 19, 2013 *https://www.foreignaffairs.com/articles/lebanon/2013-11-19/hezbollah-under-fire.*

Christian Free Patriotic Movement (FPM) are still robust. It is also possible that other Lebanese Christian political factions could strengthen relations with Hezbollah because they see it as a credible protector against Sunni extremists—if not the only one, given the relative weakness of the Lebanese army. The chances of a broader Hezbollah-Christian rapprochement in Lebanon are not great given the lingering mistrust, at least among the right-wing Christian factions, but they could increase should the Shi'ite party endorse the recent political initiative of Lebanese Forces leader Samir Geagea, which calls for the election of his old rival and FPM chief Michel Aoun as Lebanese president. Lebanon has been without a head of state—a position traditionally reserved for Maronite Christians—for nearly 2 years because its politicians have failed to resolve a broader political crisis that has paralyzed the country. If it sanctions Geagea's move, Hezbollah will be praised by an increasing number of Lebanese Christians for helping bring political relevance back to—and, in turn, ensure self-preservation of—a long-marginalized and beleaguered Christian community in Lebanon.[6]

Assad's fate notwithstanding, Hezbollah's ties to Iran will likely remain intact, though the relationship will have to adapt to its changing environment. Unlike its pragmatic relationship with Syria, Hezbollah's organic partnership with Iran is based on deep trust and shared values and interests. Hezbollah looks for ideological and strategic guidance from Iran's Supreme Leader Ayatollah Ali Khamenei, who instructs his regime's intelligence institutions and elite military units to work closely with Hezbollah. Hezbollah has acquired more autonomy from Iran since the 1980s, and may currently be considered more of a partner than a surrogate, but the group still relies on Iranian training, weapons, and funding. While the overall numbers are unknown, the group likely receives anywhere between $100 million and $200 million annually from Iran—and this number often goes up in times of need.

The shared interest of these two actors ensures that this relationship will survive in some form, regardless of the outcome of events in Syria. However, how the Iranian regime responds to changing dynamics in Syria will directly affect Hezbollah's future. Iran could instruct Hezbollah to continue the fight in Syria to try to maintain supply routes and create new allies. Hezbollah could also see itself assume a greater regional role in the service of Iranian interests, to compensate for the loss of Syria (Iraq is one obvious place where it might act given Hezbollah's long-standing links to Shi'a groups there and Iran's strong interests in Iraq). But all of this would come at the risk of overstretch, which could weaken Hezbollah at home. Not only would Hezbollah have to protect itself against a much more hostile environment in Syria, but it would also need to potentially guard against opportunistic local political actors who could exploit its relative weakness. While Hezbollah offers many benefits to Iran, including loyalty to its revolutionary ideology and projection of Shi'ite power in Arab lands, its biggest value is its military arsenal, which could be used in the event that Israel launches a war against Iran.

Hezbollah made war and war made Hezbollah. In conflict after conflict, the organization has proven its prowess and shown itself a notch above other Middle Eastern militant groups—and even Arab state militaries. From 1985 to 2000, Hezbollah forces battled Israel in the security zone along the Israeli border, inflicting a steady stream of casualties that eventually led Israel to withdraw, marking the first time Arab arms defeated Israeli arms. Hezbollah has also launched rockets at Israel, and as the range of its weapons systems expanded, so did the concern of Israeli leaders. In 2006, Israel and Hezbollah fought for more than a month, with Hezbollah killing more than 160 Israelis—heavy losses for the small and casualty-sensitive Jewish state. During the fight, Hezbollah demonstrated its military strength, ambushing Israeli armored forces and maintaining a rocket barrage in the face of Israeli air strikes and ground incursion. Hezbollah's population surged in the aftermath of that war, with its leader, Hassan Nasrallah, briefly becoming the most admired man in the Arab world.

After the 2006 war and until the outbreak of the Syrian conflict, Hezbollah focused militarily on Israel, as both sides feared another war would break out. Iran helped rearm Hezbollah, making it even more formidable than before and replenishing (and improving) its rocket arsenals. Hezbollah training camps have models of Israeli streets and the organization otherwise prepares its forces for taking on Israel. Hezbollah maintains a vast network of tunnels to hide its forces and rocket launchers as well as secure communications, all in preparation for an Israeli strike. Hezbollah has roughly 20,000 men under arms, of which 5,000 are elite fighters.

[6] Bilal Y. Saab, "Back to Lebanon's Future: The Political Revival of the Country's Christians," *Foreign Affairs*, January 26, 2016 *https://www.foreignaffairs.com/articles/lebanon/2016-01-26/back-lebanons-future.*

Hezbollah can call on thousands more in a pinch; it has deliberately kept the size of its forces limited to ensure a high level of training and commitment.

Hezbollah began to intervene militarily in Syria in 2012. This was limited at first, but the growing desperation of the Assad regime forced Hezbollah to step up its involvement and justify its role. The Shi'ite group has sustained heavy losses, with perhaps a thousand dead and many more wounded, and veteran commanders counted among the casualties. Roughly 5,000 Hezbollah soldiers fight at a time, but the organization regularly rotates its forces to spread the burden evenly. Nevertheless, to keep its numbers up, Hezbollah deploys younger recruits who are obviously less experienced in warfare. Hezbollah has also changed its tactics. In battles in and around the Syrian town of Qusair in 2013, Hezbollah took heavy casualties as its forces directly assaulted dug-in Syrian rebel positions. In subsequent operations in the Qalamoun mountain area, however, Hezbollah forces slowly advanced and even let some rebels escape, in order to minimize further casualties.

Hezbollah's fighting experience in Syria, while costly in terms of lives and resources, has provided numerous military benefits. Hezbollah is now a larger fighting force by at least 20 percent (although 15 percent of the initial size is now operating in Syria), skilled in both conventional and urban warfare. The demands of war in Syria has made it more effective in recruiting soldiers from its own constituency and others, and subsequently in training them. Thousands of younger volunteers have undergone training in recent years in camps in southern Lebanon.[7] The training lasts anywhere between 2 to 3 months and focuses on street battle and counterinsurgency tactics.

POLICY IMPLICATIONS AND RECOMMENDATIONS

Hezbollah is exhausted and perhaps overwhelmed, but it also sees light at the end of the Syrian tunnel. Equally important, it does not seem like its adversaries, domestic and foreign alike, are in a position to take advantage of its present struggles or make its life more difficult. This makes Hezbollah's uncertain transition from domestic hegemon to regional powerhouse less perilous and more achievable.

In Lebanon, pro-Western and anti-Syrian politicians are unlikely to gain from Hezbollah's travails. They are divided within, and have shown themselves unable to sustain mass support. Rather, it is militia leaders and extremists who are likely to grow more powerful. The more than 1.2 million Syrian refugees in Lebanon—a little more than a quarter of the total population—are a wild card. They might become radicalized, and their camps could become a sanctuary for fighters in Syria. It is even possible that, over time, they might become a violent player in Lebanon's politics itself, as the Palestinians did before them. This is a particular concern for Hezbollah, as the majority of the refugees in Lebanon are Sunni Muslims who see Hezbollah as the friend of their enemy.

In Israel, some in the government might see opportunity in launching a devastating attack against Hezbollah at a time when it appears vulnerable and overstretched. The country's military leadership also is keeping a close eye on the threat posed by the group's new albeit modest presence in the Israeli-occupied Golan Heights. But most of Israel's generals have no appetite for another round of fighting with Hezbollah. That is because they realize that the potential costs of such a military adventure and the risk of catastrophic escalation have dramatically increased.

Hezbollah is battle-weary and it cannot easily take on a new foe, especially one such as the Israel Defense Forces (IDF). But it is also battle-hardened. As previously mentioned, the group has learned new tricks, and it has been warning since the end of the last conflict in August 2006 that should there be another war, it will conduct cross-border operations—a new element to its military strategy.[8] Hassan Nasrallah's threat to dispatch units into Galilee bolsters his previous carefully-phrased warnings of what Israel can expect from Hezbollah in the next war. Those include a vow in February 2010 to rocket Tel Aviv's Ben Gurion airport if Israel bombs Beirut's international airport, in addition to a declaration by Nasrallah 3 months later that his group can and will attack shipping along Israel's entire coastline if the Israeli navy shells Lebanese infrastructure. That the range of Hezbollah's rockets and missiles puts all of Israel in danger makes Nasrallah's threats more credible.

The border with Israel has been quiet since 2006, and the drain of the Syrian conflict makes Hezbollah even more cautious. Israel, for its part, is trying to walk a

---

[7] Bassem Mroue, "Hezbollah recruiting push comes amid deeper role in Syria," *Associated Press*, December 18, 2015 *http://bigstory.ap.org/article/de8588cd81244ed58a7dd12e32ee18e2/hezbollah-recruiting-push-covers-its-deeper-role-syria.*

[8] Nicholas Blanford and Bilal Y. Saab, "Hezbollah on Offense," *The National Interest*, March 8, 2011 *http://nationalinterest.org/commentary/hezbollah-offense-4982.*

fine line. On the one hand, it wants to prevent transfers of Syrian and Iranian arms to Hezbollah, particularly for systems like surface-to-air missiles, anti-ship cruise missiles, or even chemical weapons that might significantly increase the threat to Israel. To that end, it has at times attacked Hezbollah forces transferring weapons, leading Hezbollah to conduct limited attacks on the Golan Heights in response, using Syrian territory as a base. On the other hand, Israel is in no mood for a broader clash that could involve Iran. Too many strikes on Hezbollah, or forcing Hezbollah into a position where its political standing depends on a fight with Israel, would be a self-defeating action for Israel, bringing on the war it hopes to deter.

Nevertheless, conflict might still break out: Few predicted the 2006 war, for example. Given that Israel regularly hits Hezbollah weapons shipments, the chances of escalation remain considerable. Israel might miscalculate about whether a particular strike would result in escalation, while Hezbollah might think a limited response would not lead Israel to up the ante. Much would depend on the domestic political position of both the Israeli government and of Hezbollah, and neither one has shown much aptitude for understanding the other's politics. In addition, Hezbollah has positioned its forces to help Iran deter Israel. Should Iran become embroiled in a conflict involving Israel, Hezbollah is prepared to act. Of all the unknowns regarding the next war, the one certainty is that it will be of such magnitude and lethality that it will make the month-long confrontation of 2006 look like a Sunday afternoon stroll in the park.

There is no end in sight to the conflict in Syria, and the growing sectarianism and risk of violence in Lebanon will put Syrian jihadists—not America or Israel—at the center of Hezbollah's radar, regardless of its rhetoric. The military drain of keeping thousands of fighters in supply and well-trained will crowd out other organizational priorities, and Hezbollah will be perceived as even more of a sectarian actor in Lebanon. Hezbollah will have to rely more on rockets and para-military activities as an asymmetric response.

Hezbollah does maintain its capacity for acting internationally. In recent years, Hezbollah used terrorist tactics to respond to what it sees as Israeli aggression against itself or against Iran. For example, Hezbollah is suspected to have struck Israel and Jewish facilities in Argentina in the 1990s, in response to what it considered Israeli escalation in the border war in Lebanon. Hezbollah also is believed to have attempted several international terrorist attacks against Israeli targets in Europe and Asia after Israel allegedly killed Imad Mughniyeh in 2008, the Shi'ite party's most senior military commander and head of external operations.

Despite Hezbollah's role in terrorism and anti-American rhetoric, the organization, by default, shares several interests with the United States—though both sides would be loath to admit it. Both actors are at war with the Islamic State and other Sunni extremists, and both want to prop up Iraqi Prime Minister Haidar Abadi's government in Baghdad. Even within Lebanon, while Washington supports Hezbollah's political rivals in the anti-Syrian March 14 coalition, it recognizes that Hezbollah is helping hold the country together, and that either an Islamic State expansion or a descent into chaos would be worse than the status quo. Open cooperation, however, is politically out of the question and not desirable for both parties. Indeed, a slight shift could turn suspicion into conflict.

The U.S.-led coalition in Syria is focused on Sunni extremists, and thus is indirectly helping the Assad regime, Hezbollah's ally. Yet, if Washington decides to live up to its anti-Assad rhetoric and take on the Syrian regime as well as Sunni jihadists, it will also be taking on Hezbollah. Hezbollah's hostility to Israel remains strong, another point of friction. In addition, Hezbollah is more in bed with Iran now than ever before, and any military action against Tehran must seriously factor in Hezbollah's response.

Any serious assessment of Hezbollah's terrorist threat to the U.S. homeland, and whether it might increase or decrease following the lifting of international sanctions against Iran, must look at both the intentions and capabilities of the group. Nobody in the U.S. Government doubts the group's terrorist capabilities. Indeed, there is a healthy appreciation within the U.S. intelligence community for what Hezbollah is capable of. But it is on the issue of intentions where there might be some debate, although the overwhelming majority of analysts and officials I have known and briefed on Hezbollah throughout my career concur that the group has no interest in striking on U.S. soil.

While Hezbollah did hit U.S. interests in the region, it has never launched an attack on U.S. territory. Two main factors explain this record: First, Hezbollah's international activities are strictly controlled by Iranian paramilitary and intelligence agencies. Indeed, Hezbollah's so-called external operations wing is an extension of the Iranian Quds Force. So, Hezbollah neither strategizes nor acts alone when it comes to global operations. It does so under the strategic guidance and close supervision of Iran. In short, the "Hezbollah international terrorism problem" is, essentially, an "Iran international terrorism problem." In other words, with Hezbollah, unlike terror caused by the Islamic State and al-Qaeda, there is a clear return address, and it is Tehran. Second, Hezbollah has no interest in perpetuating terrorism directly against the United States, and is fully aware of both its limitations and the steep price it would pay for attacking the United States. This is a fight it has no desire in picking.

Could the group's calculus with regard to the United States change in the foreseeable future? A lot would depend on the evolution of relations between the United States and Iran. While there is some alignment of interests in the Middle East between the 2 countries, and inter-governmental communication seems to be improving following the conclusion of the Nuclear Deal, ties are still tense and unpredictable due to high mistrust and many other conflicting interests in the region. Should relations take a dramatic turn for the worse over escalation following, for example, a grave incident at sea in the Arab Gulf; an inadvertent clash on the ground in Iraq or elsewhere; or a violation by Tehran of the Nuclear Deal—Iran, due to its massive conventional inferiority relative to the United States, might employ asymmetric tools and particularly terrorism to defend itself in the event of confrontation. Hezbollah could very well be one of those tools. But even under this scenario, Hezbollah would still weigh its options and think twice before deciding to take on the most powerful nation on earth.

Hezbollah is officially designated by the U.S. Government as a terrorist organization. Therefore, there are clear constraints regarding what Washington can do with the party. In essence, the United States does not have a policy toward the group beyond refusing to directly talk to or deal with it. As I wrote almost 6 years ago,[9] the most effective strategic option the United States can and should pursue with regard to Hezbollah is containment. At the end of the day, the party is a product of Lebanon's internal weakness; Iran's intervention in Lebanese domestic politics; and the on-going conflict with Israel. The United States has neither the desire nor the capacity to solve all these complex problems on its own. The best thing it can do is continue to help build state capacity in Lebanon and bolster the country's internal strength by providing military assistance to the Lebanese Armed Forces. This process of state-building, should it produce tangible and lasting results, would ultimately weaken Hezbollah's rationale for keeping its arms.

Mr. KING. Thank you, Mr. Saab.

I thank all of you for your testimony.

My first question will be to you, Mr. Saab: Do you think it is just that Iran is just a patron of Hezbollah? I mean, how much control does Iran have over Hezbollah? Assume there is a crisis between the United States and Iran. Could Iran direct Hezbollah to carry out an attack?

You said Hezbollah, it would have to decide whether or not they want to take action against the United States. How much leeway would they have if Iran came down and said, "We want you to do this?"

Mr. SAAB. That is an interesting question. I believe that, over time, Hezbollah has gained some kind of autonomy from its main patron, but only on specific issues. Those do not include global operations. So, on those issues, I would say there is a lot of room for maneuvering for the organization, politically, inside Lebanon. They run their own show in Lebanon, to be honest.

As far as regional interventions and the intervention in Syria, I would say there is significant pressure coming from Tehran, asking it to intervene on its behalf to save the regime of the Syrian president.

As far as global operations, I would say they work in consultation, very, very closely. If they were to be asked to intervene glob-

[9] Bilal Y. Saab, *Levantine Reset: Toward A More Viable U.S. Strategy For Lebanon*, Analysis Paper, Number 21 (Washington, DC: Brookings Institution, July 2010) *http://www.brookings.edu//media/research/files/papers/2010/7/lebanon-saab/07_lebanon_saab.-pdf.*

ally on their behalf, I would say that, yes, they would think about it twice.

But, at the end of the day, the partnership is too strong. This source of support is so crucial for its own survival and its own well-being, that I would suspect, at the end of the day, that they would basically accept whatever the Iranians would ask them to do, on a global level.

Mr. KING. Could that include an attack on the homeland?

Mr. SAAB. It is gonna be a tough decision, but if it really comes down to this, and we witness a serious escalation of relations between Iran and the United States, there is growing regional instability, everything is at stake, I suspect so, sir.

Mr. KING. I would like to, I guess, ask all of the witnesses this. As I said, I opposed the Iran agreement. But, quite frankly, I thought we would at least see 6 months to a year of good behavior on Iran's part, at least to go through the motions to show that there was some salutary effect from this agreement, that Iran was going to try to become a respected member of the community of nations.

Yet, as you mentioned, they seem to be going out of their way, you know, since the agreement was reached, to almost provoke the United States, probably most notably with the seizure of the sailors and then today, I said, you know, the release of the photos.

First of all, I will ask you, were you surprised by that? Second, what is their intention in doing this?

Mr. KAHN. Well, thank you for that question. Unfortunately, I am not surprised by that. I think there is, actually, a very simple reason that Iran has continued its aggression, because I think it knows that it can do so. They know that they are unlikely to suffer meaningful consequences for doing so.

After all, Iran now has extraordinary leverage over us. They understand how important the Nuclear Deal is to us, and they know full well that we will take dramatic steps to ensure its survival. We will be willing to tolerate an extraordinary amount of aggression on its part, if we had to choose between the deal and stopping its regional aggression.

So I think Iran has recognized that, and I think its ruthlessly exploiting it. So I don't think this should really come as too much of a surprise.

Mr. BERMAN. I agree completely with Mr. Kahn. I think there is an argument to be made, even if one is a proponent of the Nuclear Deal, that it could have been negotiated more judiciously, to spread out the economic benefit that Iran receives over the lifetime, over the next decade, the lifetime of the agreement.

As it stands, Iran has received, already, and is receiving the lion's share of economic benefit from the JCPOA, both in terms of the near-term cash infusion of the $100 billion that have been released, but also of the rush by countries in Europe and countries in Asia to re-engage with Iran on non-oil trade, which is going to stabilize the Iranian economy further, as we move into the future.

This provides, I think, economic backing for precisely the political calculus that Mr. Kahn talked about, which is that the Iranians understand that, while empirically they are the weaker party in this negotiation, for political reasons the administration is far more invested in the preservation of this agreement then the Iranian regime, itself, actually is. As a result, they feel like they can act with relative impunity.

Mr. KING. Mr. Saab.

Mr. SAAB. Mr. Chairman, I have little to add to those excellent responses. I would just emphasize the fact that, you know, the Iranian regime has had some interesting divisions within it.

I wasn't really surprised by what happened with the sailors, because those types of activities—and its—typically, its regional involvements and its foreign policy are—is controlled by, I hate the terms, hardline and moderate. It is all relative. It is more like those who really oppose the deal and those who endorse it.

Those still control Iranian foreign policy. How that tension plays out in the foreseeable future is something really worth watching, for sure.

Mr. KING. Okay. Mr. Higgins.

Mr. HIGGINS. Thank you, very much.

First on the issue of the Nuclear Deal, and I think, however imperfect it is, the objective is something that everybody agreed with, and that is bolstering deterrents, keeping Iran from having that breakout capability.

Prior to the deal, it was estimated that the breakout time was a couple of months. Under the deal, it appears to be about a year, perhaps more, over a 15-year period. A lot of speculation, justifiably so, and skepticism about what happens after that 15-year period.

A couple of notes on that. Dennis Ross and David Petraeus advanced an argument that the administration should provide Israel with additional weapons, toward the goal of bolstering deterrents in the region, keeping Iran in check, relative to what their regional ambitions may be.

In doing so, they specifically referenced a 30,000-pound massive ordinance penetrator, otherwise known as MOP, and the means to carry it, be it a B–2 or a B–52. First of all, your thoughts on that? Anybody or everybody.

Mr. KAHN. I think that would be a wise course of action. As I said, Iran is doing what it is doing, because it knows and it feels that it is in charge. It feels that it can get away with it.

I think, if we are going to effect a change in Iranian behavior, we need to change their cost-benefit analysis. We need to send them the message that there will be meaningful consequences for their actions.

I think, to raise those stakes for them, to send them that message, I think it would be very wise for us to empower and strengthen our allies in the region, such as Israel, in order to tell them that, if they do try something aggressive, there may very well be significant consequences.

Mr. BERMAN. Congressman Higgins, I take your point on the Nuclear Deal and, sort of, the comparative merits and the flaws therein. I would only point out that, as I try to lay out in my written statement, what we are looking at is a deal that has a scope that is intended by the administration to be tactical and, yet, benefits for the Iranian regime that are truly strategic in nature.

That imbalance, I think, empowers a great deal of the skepticism about the long-term benefit of the deal, vis-á-vis the balance between the United States and Iran. The second point, on the additional weapons for Israel, I concur, as far as it goes. However, that doesn't amount to a strategy for dealing with Iran.

Certainly, it is necessary to provide reassurances to not only Israel, but also our allies in the Gulf, that they are more capable than they were before of preventing rising Iranian aggression or rising Iranian adventurism.

But that shouldn't be seen as a substitute for having a strategy, an American strategy, for managing the consequences of the deal, because, while the debate over the agreement, as you know, in this chamber and in others, over the summer, was very rancorous, the deal has passed.

We are now looking at a situation where, over the next several years, the impact of the agreement is going to put certain Iranian behaviors into play. Our job, I believe, is to track those behaviors and to craft a strategy to respond to them. Such weapon supplies may be part of that strategy, but they are not the sum total.

Mr. SAAB. Fully agree with Mr. Berman's assertion. I would like to remind you, Mr. Higgins, that, you know, Iran is conventionally inferior, in many ways, relative to our partners in the Gulf and also to Israel. They feel, one of the missile defenses in the world, even though Iran's ballistic missile capabilities are growing.

I think that there is a good understanding among officials in the Department of Defense that deterrence on that level is working just fine. Now, where we have done not a very good job is at deterring Iran from actually using its asymmetric tools in the region. Now, they have been pretty good at that.

That requires, exactly like Mr. Berman said, a comprehensive strategy. They have been quite effective at it for a very long time, and there is a reason why they use it. It is because, once again, they are inferior when it comes to conventional capabilities.

A lot of ways that our partners in the Gulf could respond to that. I think it starts, really, with internal strength, building their special operations forces. I think they finally get it. Mr. Carter has been emphasizing this for quite some time. His message has been well-received. But it will take time. It will take time, because they are not really used to that.

Mr. HIGGINS. Yes. Let me ask you this. You guys are relatively young, you know, well-schooled in this region, its politics, its history. You don't buy the argument that Iran has the potential to change over the next 10 years?

I mean, you really look at the hardliners, which is not a majority of the population, but they probably, at the moment, disproportionately influence the politics of Iran and how that is communicated to the Western world.

But there is also an argument that Iran, a population of 80 million people, feels humiliated the rest of the world has moved on, beyond them, fairly well-educated, young.

You know, Rouhani, he really is a reformer. Now, I am not saying that, you know, a reformer within, you know, the Western tradition, but clearly a reformer. He ran against the policies that created sanctions in the first place. The Supreme Leader, Khamenei, certainly could have forced a runoff, given the corrupt nature of the politics in Iran. He didn't. Rouhani was elected and said that the economic situation was even worse than he thought it was, as a candidate, upon taking election, taking office.

So I just think, you know, it is not, you know, it is not black and white. There are no absolutes there. You know, there is—you know, I think you have gotta take a nuanced approach to it.

You listen to the young scholars coming out of Iran, they speak of an Iran that wants to be part of the rest of the world, economically, culturally, and otherwise, because, you know, social media, Twitter, the internet is not only used for, you know, organizational purposes, in helping to create revolutions, but, also, for aspirational purposes.

So, even more, young people are seeing how everybody else is living, and they want to be part of that. So I think we are at a real critical time in Iranian history and politics, as to what Iran is going to be in the next 10 years.

Just a final thought on this. I saw where, you know, the father of the revolution, his grandson was trying to get into the general assembly, which selects the supreme leader. He was rejected, Khomenei. They said that he was too young and too inexperienced. The average age of the assembly that selects the supreme leader is 80.

Well, at the conclusion of this Nuclear Deal, Iran could be a very different place, with different leaders who have a different view of what, ultimately, Iran wants to be in the future.

I know I went over.

Mr. KAHN. I think you raise a very important question, but I think if you look at how events have actually unfolded, since President Rouhani has came to power, there is really very little evidence to suggest that he is a reformer in any meaningful sense.

Human rights abuses in the country has, arguably, gotten worse over the least 2 years. Iran still executes more people per capita than almost any other country in the world. There has been no improvement, in terms of freedom of speech, in terms of freedom of religion.

Iranians are still routinely imprisoned, in Iran's notorious prisons, for simply speaking their mind, for practicing their religion, for criticizing the regime. These are things that are still the norm in Iran today.

So I don't see it. So, despite the image that I think President Rouhani has taken great pains to cultivate during this time, as a reformer, the policies in the regime have really not reflected that aspiration.

I would also point out that, even if President Rouhani were inclined to make the kinds of reforms we would like to see, his ability to do so is actually fairly limited. The chief entities responsible for Iran's regional aggression and domestic oppression is the Islamic Revolutionary Guard Corps, also known as, basically, the regime's Praetorian Guard.

They don't report to President Rouhani. They report to Supreme Leader Ali Khamenei. In the end, President Rouhani's power is, really, as a result, very fairly limited. Therefore, I think it is a mistake to suggest that the current regime has really changed in any way.

I see very little evidence to suggest that that change is really on the horizon. I think, in fact, when you look at how the regime—the regime's aggression has increased both domestically and abroad, just in the 7 months since the Nuclear Deal, I think that creates a very grim picture.

I think it is, unfortunately, a warning of things to come, to which I would also add one final point, which is that, you know, over the last 7 months, Iran really had every incentive to stay on the good side of the international community, because they hadn't yet received sanctions relief.

So you would have thought that, given how much of an incentive they had to stay on the good side of the West, they would have, perhaps, restrained themselves. But, in fact, they have not done so.

I think that begs the question, if they are willing to provoke us in this way, when they have every incentive to not do so, how much more so are they going to be willing to provoke us when they have already received their sanctions relief and our economic leverage has dramatically diminished?

Mr. BERMAN. Mr. Higgins, if I may, I agree completely that Iran finds itself either in the midst of or at the cusp of a critical time, but I would focus on slightly different data points in explaining my views on this.

Iran is a country of 81 million people. Two-thirds of the Iranian population is under the age of 35, which means that they weren't alive at the time of the Islamic Revolution. It means that the ideological consistency of the regime wanes over time, the more people are born that do not recall Ayatollah Khomeini and the founding of the revolution.

This is significant, because what you saw in the summer of 2009, after the re-election of Mahmoud Ahmadinejad to the Iranian presidency, was really a groundswell of potential transformation, right? We are on the—we are hoping that this Nuclear Deal will precipitate lightening to strike twice, essentially, to sort-of to catalyze this sort-of grassroots movement.

But, if we look at what the Iranian regime, itself, is saying and is doing, it is very clear that they view the agreement not as a vehicle for reconciliation or moderation, but as a vehicle for strengthening precisely that ideological regime that is increasingly aged and increasingly rickety.

As a result, you are seeing the emergence of an increasing strain of ultra-nationalism within Iran. The debate is not between reformists and conservatives within Iran. It is between strains of conservatives within Iran about the true position of the Islamic Republic.

The consensus in their debate rests squarely on the fact that Iran should be, by its rights, by its historical destiny, a regional pole of power. The Iranian regime, irrespective of the tactical rhetoric that it assumes, is acting on that conviction, in the macro sense.

Mr. SAAB. Very briefly, Mr. Higgins, the story of Iran really is nothing but tragic. The fact that, as you very well-described, the population is—I don't have the most recent polls, but predominantly pro-Western, excited about the world, and everything that it offers, and then a leadership that has hijacked the country since 1979.

It is hard to really see a scenario, any time in the foreseeable future, where leadership becomes, you know, more cooperative, less hard-line in its policies, both at home and abroad. You know, if there were to be some types of changes of the leadership becoming less ideological, but still, obviously, problematic in many ways, I think a realistic scenario, and even that is still far-fetched, would be something resembling the Chinese system, less ideological, more open economically, but, of course, still, at home, politically closed.

You know, an X factor, which Mr. Berman has mentioned, is the—Mr. Khamenei, himself, the leader, the Supreme Leader, should he pass sometime soon, that is gonna create a major shock to the system. How that will unfold, I think, is definitely worth watching.

Mr. KING. Several more questions.

Brian, I know you have to leave. Did you have any more questions you want to ask?

Mr. HIGGINS. No, I am good. Thank you. Thank you.

Mr. KING. Okay. Thank you.

On the question of Syria, assuming that what the administration is looking for is that negotiations do go forward, that Russia has an influence in removing Assad or somehow getting Assad out of the picture, or at least wants to do that, how much control do you think Russia would have over Iran and Hezbollah, and bring that about, if Hezbollah did realize, or did see that it may lose a center of its operations by having Assad moved out? So, I guess, we will go across.

Mr. KAHN. Thank you for that question. I think it is important to recognize what Iran's goals really, in Syria and Iraq, are. For Iran, it is not simply a question of Sunni versus Shiites, with respect to that conflict. For Iran, it is also—a key part of that conflict is not about defeating ISIS, per se, but really, it is a matter of rivalry. They are seeking control of the same territory.

That is the key reason why Iran is involved in this conflict right now. That is the key reason that it is supporting the Assad regime. For Iran, the Assad regime provides the key foothold for its presence in—for its influence and presence in the Levant. It provides the avenue for which it can support Hezbollah.

Without that regime and without that ability, Iran's ability to exert leverage in the region, to which conflict against Israel would be dramatically reduced. So, I think that what we can expect to see over the coming weeks and over the coming months is Iran's continuing effort to ensure that the Assad regime remains in power for as long as it can.

I mean, I think it is not a coincidence that it was only 10 days after the nuclear agreement was signed, on July 14, 2015, that Qassem Soleimani, the commander of the IRGC Quds Force, traveled to Moscow to, perhaps, arrange and to have discussions about Russia's involvement in the region and its participation in the civil war.

It is not a coincidence that it happened so shortly after the Nuclear Deal, because Iran understood that the Nuclear Deal was going to give it room to expand its circle of operations and to deter meaningful consequences for its actions, given the leverage that the Nuclear Deal provided it. That is, of course, in addition to the sanction relief that the Nuclear Deal gave it.

So, I think, in the coming months, we will expect to see Iran's and Russia's partnership continue. That, of course, I think, will be very harmful, of course, and, really, serve to really prolong the civil war in Syria in a way that I think is very much—is very contrary to our interests and to the stability of the region.

Mr. KING. I can see what Iran wants, and my own belief, it is probably likely to go in the direction you are talking about. I guess, I am saying if, for whatever reason, Russia, for its own interests, decides that Assad should go, would Iran and Hezbollah—what would they do in that case?

I—basically, Iran has brought Russia in, or has encouraged Russia to be involved. What would they do if Russia, in effect, you know, goes to a policy which is against Iran's and Hezbollah's interests? We can go down the line. Mr. Kahn, you want to——

Mr. KAHN. Sure. I think we can expect to see that Iran is going to try to back the Assad regime, really, for as long as it can, regardless of Russia and Hezbollah's actions, because, as I said, for Iran, Syria is its foremost client. It is its most important regional partner, and it is the key mechanism for which influence—to exert its influence in the region.

I think, if the Assad regime were to fall, from Iran's perspective, that would be a catastrophe. I don't anticipate that simply if—obviously, if Russia were to withdraw its support for the Assad regime, I think—I don't think Iran would be particularly pleased about that. But I don't think it would necessarily, simply to please Russia, I don't think it would necessarily change its goals.

Mr. KING. Mr. Berman.

Mr. BERMAN. Mr. Chair, so, let me try to tackle this——

Mr. KING. Sure, yes.

Mr. BERMAN [continuing]. Slightly differently, from the Russian perspective. I think it is necessary to understand that Russia, in Syria, is operating from a rather complex set of variables that it is trying to solve. One of them, an overriding one, which doesn't get a lot of press, is the fact that Russia has its own Islamist problem.

Fully a quarter, the Russian Intelligence Service estimates, fully a quarter of the foreign fighters that have joined the Islamic State to date are either from the Russian Federation, itself, or from the countries of the former Soviet Union.

Russian is now the third-most popular language within the Caliphate, after Arabic and English. So, for the Russians, I think the strategy is, at least in part, to go abroad and fight those jihadists there, rather than wait for them to come home.

At the same time, the Russians are affected by what Iran is doing. It is not a coincidence that in the months running up to Qassem Soleimani's trip to Moscow, to visit with Vladimir Putin, the Syrian regime had lost something like one-sixth of its territory, of the territory that it held.

Simply put, Iranian support was insufficient for Assad to hold the line, and Russian assistance was necessary. So, this, I think, sets up a paradigm, by which the Russian government is involved in Syria in a way that, at least in the near term, is intended to prop up the Assad regime.

Over the longer term, the Russians want a settlement, whether Assad is part of it or not, that is favorable to their interests, including to their Islamist problem. Whether or not that mitigates in favor of continued Russian-Iranian cooperation over the long term, over Syria, I think remains to be seen. It certainly is generating cooperation now, and there may be competition later.

Mr. KING. Thank you.

Mr. Saab.

Mr. SAAB. Very briefly, Mr. Chairman. What are the Russian red lines and what are the Iranian red lines in Syria? I am not an expert, really, on Russia, but I will just provide some thoughts.

For the Iranians, I really think it is a friendly regime in Damascus that preserves the supply lines to Hezbollah and the weapons depots that it has stored inside Syria. It is really crucial for the Iranians for Hezbollah to play a potent military deterrent role vis-á-vis Israel, and the Syrian connection is quite important.

I think the Syrian president is quite salvageable. I don't think, really, it is critical for the Iranians, or the Russians, as a matter of fact, for him to stay in power. It is just that, for now, it is much easier to keep him, because he has preserved their interests quite nicely.

If there were to be an alternative that would provide the same set of services, I think that they would be amenable to that, of course, on the condition that the price that they are asking for would be met.

What are the Russian red lines? I agree with Mr. Berman. I think it is a government in Damascus that fights terrorist groups, to have links to rebels in Chechnya. Any other consideration, really, is a preference of Russia, not really a core priority.

There has been this argument that we might have, you know, the capacity to try to create a wedge between the Iranians and the Russians in Syria and try to exploit any gap between the two. Quite frankly, we haven't done a very good job at it thus far, for, I think, two reasons.

One, it is not that easy, really, to define and identify what is the gap between the two. I think there is a nice division of labor here, between the Iranians and the Russians, in terms of their activities in Syria. One is committing ground troops, the other is, obviously, by air power.

There seems to be quite an intense consultation between the 2 countries about the future of the country, as Mr. Berman has described.

Mr. KING. Thank you.

If I could bring you back to the United States. I guess it was 2011 when there was the attempted—or the planned attack in Washington on the Saudi ambassador and blowing up the restaurant, et cetera.

Has there been any conventional wisdom among the intelligence community, excuse me, that Iran would not attempt an attack here in the homeland? Obviously, there was one at that time planned.

Do you see circumstances in the immediate future, or even in the near future, where Iran would be willing to carry out an attack on the U.S. homeland?

Mr. KAHN. I think what we could expect to see more is an effort on Iran's part to engage in more incremental provocations. I don't think Iran is necessarily interested in triggering the kind of conflict—or to say engaging in a provocation that would force the United States to—that force it politically to have a strong response.

I think what we will see, instead, is a sense of a symmetry, of a symmetric conflict. In other words, if you look at the kind of things Iran has been doing, over the last 7 months, from the ballistic missile tests to the captures of the U.S. sailors, these are actions that are an effort to humiliate the United States, to exert its authority, to say that the United States is not going to be able to influence them.

But they are not the kind of things which are, necessarily, going to trigger a full-scale conflict. I don't think Iran is, necessarily, interested right now in having that kind of full-scale conflict.

So I think what we—is more likely is that we are going to continue to see more like a war of attrition, smaller-scale steps that would wear down the United States over time without triggering a kind of full-scale conflict.

Having said all that, you know, you never know. It is certainly possible that Iran could miscalculate. It is certainly possible that, if there is a new—the next president will have a different sense of strategic calculations, in terms of the way it wants to respond to Iran. That, in turn, could affect Iran's calculus.

So I wouldn't rule anything out. I think we can expect to see Iran not take the kind of steps that would be too spectacular or too catastrophic, but one which would still keep the United States on its toes and threaten its interests in the region in a very provocative way.

Mr. BERMAN. Mr. Chairman, I actually think that that is one of the most germane questions to ask in the context of the authorities of this committee, of this subcommittee. As we are looking at Iran's capabilities to hold American interests and hold the U.S. homeland at risk, I think it is necessary to go back to that incident that you mentioned, the October 2011 attempted assassination of Saudi envoy Adel al-Jubeir, here in Washington.

The debate that was generated, as a result, centered, I think, a great deal on Iranian decision making. How—what was Iran doing? Was this simply brinksmanship? Did Iran miscalculate? I think that is a fundamental misreading of how the Iranian Supreme Leader wields power.

The Iranian supreme leader is not a micromanager. He is a balancer. You see this, as he plays off different factions within his own body politics, but you also see this by—because the Iranian military, both the conventional military, the Artesh, and the clerical army, the Revolutionary Guard, tend to act in ways broadly consonant with what they think the supreme leader wants.

The attack against—or the attempted plot to assassinate Adel al-Jubeir was carried out by elements of the Revolutionary Guard, resident in Latin America, working through the Los Zetas cartel in Mexico.

That was not an order that was dictated down from Tehran, but it was certainly an order that was inspired by what the regional IRGC commanders thought the supreme leader wanted.

I think, this gets us to where we are today. What I am concerned about, looking at the track record of Iranian behavior since the passage of the JCPOA, is that it hasn't instilled a climate of cooperation, of reconciliation with the West. It has instilled a climate of defiance. Iran is trying to demonstrate that it is a regional hegemon and is willing to act globally against American interests.

In that climate, it is very possible that elements, operational elements of Iranian proxies, including Hezbollah, may take it upon themselves to try to operationalize what they think the Supreme Leader wants.

The potential for miscalculation and the potential for danger there, I think, is probably more significant than we acknowledge.

Mr. SAAB. Well, as you know, Mr. Chairman, the intelligence community will tell you that we can't predict the future, but we can try to reduce the uncertainty. So it is, certainly, not unthinkable that this would happen, but I would still say that is unlikely, for a number of reasons.

As I mentioned in my earlier testimony, it is primarily something like this would happen as a result of really massive escalation in political relations between Iran and the United States. Let me just mention a couple of scenarios.

Maybe an incident at sea, in the Iranian Gulf, that would escalate. All of a sudden, it is existential stakes for Iran. It would lash out. Given its massive conventional inferiority, it would use terrorism, whether it is in the homeland or core U.S. strategic interests abroad.

Maybe an inadvertent clash on the ground in Iraq or elsewhere, or maybe even a clear violation by Iran of the Nuclear Deal. Of course, we would have to respond to that. Then one thing leads to another.

What happened in Washington with the attempt at the life of the Saudi ambassador, quite frankly, to me, it was very surprising. It was a very bold operation. Thank God, it was foiled. Could this happen again? Possibly.

It is not really an insignificant detail to say that the target was not a U.S. strategic target. It was a Saudi official. Of course, again, in Washington, in a very crowded area, which, once again, was very surprising to me, the fact that they had decided to pull that off in the heart of the capital.

But this is, once again, this is a very pragmatic regime that is very much aware of its own vulnerabilities and its own limitations. Now, could the voices that are the most extreme in Iran call the shots for something like this? It is certainly possible, but, once again, I would say it would result following clear and very dangerous escalation between the two sides, over a number of scenarios that I just mentioned to you.

Mr. KING. At least publicly, there has been the consensus in the intelligence community and the law enforcement community, I believe, that Hezbollah, in this country, is mainly fundraising, at this stage, that they are not overtly planning attacks within the United States.

Assuming, for whatever reason, let's say there was a number of top Iranian officials were killed and the Iranians believed the U.S. was behind it, or the world thought the United States was behind it, is there a button they can press to unleash Hezbollah on this country?

In other words, is Hezbollah—do you believe there are Hezbollah elements in this country, who could respond to an order from Iran? Attack within this country, not our interests overseas, our interests here?

Mr. SAAB. Sure. Their presence has been well-documented. I am very well aware of what law enforcement agencies in the United States have been laser-focused on Hezbollah's presence, whether it is sympathizers or members. Really hard to tell a difference sometimes.

Once again, I really cannot speak with any degree of confidence to what extent, you know, Hezbollah would be willing to perpetrate such an escalatory act of political violence in the United States.

I would suspect that the preferred course of action that Iran would pursue would be an attack outside the United States, just because it is less escalatory. At the end of the day, there is a very clear return address, as far as Iranian terrorism, unlike, you know, the Islamic State, al-Qaeda. It is like chasing shadows. With Iran, it is very clear. We know where it is coming from, and they know that we know.

So, this type of understanding, in some ways, limits what they can do. But, once again, who knows what minds will prevail in Tehran. It is really hard to tell. This is a very opaque regime. Frankly, it is beyond my area of expertise what Hezbollah's international activities are.

I tend to agree with you, that, primarily, their presence in the United States and the activities that they are engaged in is fundraising. But I have heard, and I have read about, a lot of the criminal and illegal activities, not just in the United States, but, as Mr. Berman said, in Latin America and in Africa and in other places, as well.

This is quite a sophisticated network, and they have been trying to build it for some time, and, I would say, with some success.

Mr. KING. Mr. Berman.

Mr. BERMAN. I think I tend to concur. It is certainly unlikely, but I don't think you can rule out the possibility. Also——

Mr. KING. Would they have the capacity, I guess, if they did want—if they were ordered to do it, and they wanted to do it, do they have a capacity to carry out attacks here in the United States? Hezbollah?

Mr. BERMAN. I think so, to a limited extent. What concerns me is, and as I have written in my written statement, a sanctions-constrained Iran succeeded in either supporting or instigating at least 3 separate plots against the U.S. homeland, including involving Hezbollah operatives, over the last decade.

So, as we move forward in time, we do have to be wary of the potential for this level of activity to increase, as a result of incidents: Incidents that happen abroad, diplomatic incidents, a breakdown of nuclear negotiations, but also of incidents that may become more likely, as a result of increased Iranian capabilities.

As Iran receives the economic benefits of reintegration into the global community, it is, I think, a very strong possibility that there will be a trickle-down effect for its terror proxies, including Hezbollah.

If Hezbollah is postured globally, including in the Western Hemisphere, as I think you have heard testimony to that effect, I think we need to be worried about what that does for Hezbollah's latent potential against the U.S. homeland, as well.

Mr. KING. Mr. Kahn.

Mr. KAHN. I concur with my colleagues, and I don't, necessarily, have that much to add, except to say that I think, again, how the United States postures itself towards Iran over the course of the implementation of the agreement will have a very big impact on how Iran calculates to what degree it will be able to survive and withstand a potential aggressive act against the United States.

The more Iran feels confident that it can get away with such behavior, or that the United States lacks the resolve to engage in a meaningful response, I think the more likely it becomes that Iran is going to be willing to risk that kind of provocation.

Now, again, I can't, you know, predict the future. Certainly, anything is possible. But I think that just, again, reinforces the need, on our part, for the United States to send that message to Iran that, should it engage in any provocation, we will respond.

To the extent that we fail to send that message, I think it increases the likelihood of further aggression.

Mr. KING. Mr. Saab, you wanted to add? Yes?

Mr. SAAB. Two things, very, very briefly. It is a very clear yes on the issue of capabilities, in case I wasn't clear on that. As I mentioned in my testimony, Hezbollah's international activities are an extension, at the end of the day, of Iranian paramilitary and intelligence agencies. Those are quite capable, themselves.

I think there is a very healthy appreciation in the U.S. Government for what Hezbollah is capable of, only because of its connection to Iranian paramilitary organizations.

Mr. KING. Okay. This will be my last question. It is for Mr. Saab, and either of you can comment on it, also.

I think, in answer to a question before, you said Hezbollah realizes that if they did confront the United States, that we could wipe them out or eliminate them. How could we do that? I am glad to hear that, but how would you see that being done?

Mr. SAAB. Well, at the end of the day, Hezbollah relies, as I mentioned before, on two critical sources of support. Those would be the relationship with Iran and a relationship with the support base.

We, obviously, have to balance between our own interests in Lebanon as a whole, as a country, and also our own policy or approach with regards to Hezbollah. Now, you know, we should ask the Israelis. There has been on-going conflict between Hezbollah and Israelis for—since 1982. There has been a lot of tactical successes by the Israelis against Hezbollah.

They have been trying to disarm the organization for a long time, but they have not been successful, for a number of reasons. I mean, this is a very deeply-rooted organization within the country.

I think what the United States could tackle very effectively is the issue of global operations, because the dialogue, and I mentioned before, the return address is Tehran. But, in terms of its own presence inside the country, it is gonna be very difficult for the United States to really mount policies that would reduce its popularity, that would disarm it.

I mean, at the end of the day, this is quite a massive military arsenal. As I mentioned, the several confrontations with Israel over the past few years, with 3 high-intensity military conflicts in 2006, 1996, 1993, none of them have actually led to the disarming of the organization. As a matter of fact, have made the organization even stronger.

So the United States can effectively tackle the issue of terrorism through Iran, but, in terms of its own local position, its own—in terms of its regional influence and all that, I mean, that is going to require quite a comprehensive strategy that the United States has not formulated, thus far.

Mr. KING. Mr. Berman.

Mr. BERMAN. I tend to disagree, Mr. Chairman. I think it is, while an optimistic idea, it is rather an impractical one to assume that we can root out Hezbollah, root and branch, and, sort-of, dismantle the organization.

I would say that there is considerable merit to focusing on, as Mr. Saab said, to focus on the global activities portion of what Hezbollah is doing. In particular, in the context of the Western Hemisphere, Hezbollah has vacillated between being an appendage of Iran, a narcoterrorist organization, and somewhere in the middle, over the last decade, depending on Iran's financial health and its subjection to intentional sanctions, as a result of its nuclear program.

I think, here, the zone of danger comes from us having less ability to discern exactly how strong Hezbollah is and what it is doing. As successive commanders of U.S. Southern Command have said, before the House Armed Services Committee, for example, the posture of SOUTHCOM, the ability of Southern Command to really see into South America and Central America to understand what these external actors, like Hezbollah, are doing, has actually diminished over time, as budgets have constricted.

That creates a possibility that Hezbollah and, by extension, Iran, has the potential to grow exponentially, without being watched, without being seen by the U.S. intelligence community, by the U.S. military. That creates a potential for, I think, a very dangerous synergy with local radicals, with local criminal organizations, that isn't really being adequately addressed. That would be the place that I would start, if I was to begin focusing on Hezbollah's global activities.

Hezbollah has entrenched itself south of our border, over the last 3 decades. It has carried out terrorist attacks south of our border, over the last 3 decades. It has begun, increasingly, to reach northward including into the U.S. homeland from there.

That may be, for our intents and purposes, that may be the most functional place to start, if we think about addressing Hezbollah globally.

Mr. KING. Mr. Kahn.

Mr. KAHN. I concur with Mr. Berman, and, to which I would also add, I think there is, of course, I don't think, any realistic way to simply wipe out Hezbollah. But I think it goes back to the point that I discussed earlier, which is that, you know, I think if we have to—if we want to weaken Hezbollah, we have to weaken its patron.

In the end, if Iran possesses the ability to continue sponsoring Hezbollah, then I think we can only continue to expect that it will grow, and its power will remain as is. So, in the end, if—if our goal is to reduce the influence of Hezbollah, we really have to focus on reducing the ability of Iran to keep it in power. I think that really has to be our focus, if our goal is to reduce Hezbollah's influence.

Mr. KING. Let me thank all the witnesses. If anyone has anything to add, they certainly can. But I want to thank you for your testimony here today. You have certainly taken a very complex situation and applied a level of coherence to it that we haven't had before.

So I want to thank you for that, and just want to state for the record that the Members of this subcommittee may have additional questions for the witnesses. We would ask you to respond to those in writing. Any of the Members, especially those who were not here, and pursuant to committee rule 7(e), the hearing record will be held open for 10 days.

Without objection, the subcommittee stands adjourned.

[Whereupon, at 11:17 a.m., the subcommittee was adjourned.]

○